Give it a Grow

'Martha invites us to think of gardening the way we do cooking – imperfectly, joyfully and learning as we go. I've never felt so compelled to get into my garden. It was a true joy to read' Yotam Ottolenghi

'A truly inspiring book' Nigella Lawson

'If there was ever a book to inspire people to grow their own food, this is it. Martha's "just crack on" approach, and the charming story of her own love affair with her veg plot, is by turns empowering, cajoling and irresistibly enticing. In the end you just can't say no. And why would you? Everything this book is celebrating just makes life better – for you and the world around you' Hugh Fearnley-Whittingstall

'How to grow it, how to eat it – this is my kind of book!' Jasmine Hemsley

'Martha's love and knowledge of food stems from her passion for gardening. From delicate edible flowers to robust hearty root vegetables, this book will guide and inspire you to grow your own and have some fun on the way' Michel Roux

'You don't have to be naturally green-fingered to love this book. It's friendly, easy to read and even easier to understand. But most of all it will make you want to get into the garden' Nadiya Hussain

'Martha has been inspiring me for years with her clever, creative and super-practical ideas and now she's gathered them into one beautiful and practical guide. I'm such a fan boy, it's kinda embarrassing' James Wong

'I especially love where Martha describes how we can all be gardeners without having gardens. Her approach to gardening is fun, natural and very heartfelt in this book. But I must say: Martha's enthusiasm towards gardening and connectivity to nature is a bug (pardon the pun) she picked up from her mother; that is evident in every page of this book' Rekha Mistry, Head Gardener, presenter, author

Give it a Grow

Simple Projects to Nurture Food,
Flowers and Wildlife in
Any Outdoor Space

MARTHA SWALES

Illustrations by Nina Chakrabarti

PENGUIN LIFE

AN IMPRINT OF

PENGUIN BOOKS

PENGUIN LIFE

UK | USA | Canada | Ireland | Australia
India | New Zealand | South Africa

Penguin Life is part of the Penguin Random House group of companies
whose addresses can be found at global.penguinrandomhouse.com.

Penguin Random House UK,
One Embassy Gardens, 8 Viaduct Gardens, London SW11 7BW

penguin.co.uk

First published 2025

005

Text copyright © Martha Swales, 2025
Illustrations copyright © Nina Chakrabarti, 2025

The moral right of the copyright holders has been asserted

Penguin Random House values and supports copyright.
Copyright fuels creativity, encourages diverse voices, promotes freedom
of expression and supports a vibrant culture. Thank you for purchasing
an authorized edition of this book and for respecting intellectual property
laws by not reproducing, scanning or distributing any part of it by any
means without permission. You are supporting authors and enabling
Penguin Random House to continue to publish books for everyone.
No part of this book may be used or reproduced in any manner for the
purpose of training artificial intelligence technologies or systems. In accordance
with Article 4(3) of the DSM Directive 2019/790, Penguin Random House
expressly reserves this work from the text and data mining exception.

Set in 12.25/15pt Garamond MT Pro
Typeset by Jouve (UK), Milton Keynes
Printed and bound in Great Britain by Clays Ltd, Elcograf S.p.A.

The authorized representative in the EEA is Penguin Random House Ireland,
Morrison Chambers, 32 Nassau Street, Dublin D02 YH68

A CIP catalogue record for this book is available from the British Library

ISBN: 978–0–241–71036–4

Penguin Random House is committed to a sustainable future
for our business, our readers and our planet. This book is made from
Forest Stewardship Council® certified paper.

To my mum, for giving me the gift
of gardening and all that comes with it. x

Contents

1. An introduction — 1
2. The basics — 11
3. How to grow vegetables — 57
4. How to grow herbs — 167
5. How to grow fruit — 195
6. How to nurture wildlife — 229
7. How to grow flowers — 259
8. Sit back and take it all in — 289

Acknowledgements — 293

Index — 295

I

AN INTRODUCTION

Twelve years ago, on the first sunny day of the year, I found myself at Kew Gardens. As a child I'd been before, but this was the first time I'd been there of my own volition. At the end of the afternoon I arrived in the shop, and stood transfixed in front of a huge wall of seed packets, full of potential. I picked five or six packets, more or less at random. Off I went back home to sow them – the small beginnings of what grew into an all-consuming obsession.

I've always been prone to great enthusiasm for new hobbies, and having sown my aubergine seeds and carefully placed them near the radiator, I would often sit on the floor next to them, constantly checking for signs of life. Once my seedlings raised their delicate heads above the soil, the next task was to find a home for the new lives I had ushered into being. My mum has a beautiful garden, which she has been tending with great skill and patience for over forty years. My new obsession with vegetables and her carefully landscaped and masterfully planted garden were not immediately happy bedfellows. I started with pots on the sunny deck, grow-bags, old crates lined with plastic bags, anything and everything I could find to grow food in. After running out of space on the deck, I began to spread further afield, putting large grow-bags directly on top of my mum's lawn. That summer I harvested wonky broccoli, sunshine yellow patty-pans, knobbly thick-skinned cucumbers and one very small, beautifully glossy black aubergine. Her hand having been forced, the following year my mum dug up the dismal remains of her lawn and replaced it with the most beautiful flowers: tall trumpets of nicotiana, the heady scent of valerian, elegant stems of *Verbena bonariensis*, and the vibrant pink Catherine wheel faces of red campion, all of which still grace the garden every year over a decade later.

Few things in my life have changed it as much as those seed packets from the Kew Gardens shop. Growing food is not just about harvests, although they are of course nice. The seeds grew into an enduring fascination with watching life unfold as the seasons roll by: the unpredictable turns of weather, sunshine, rain, drought, cold, with a million tiny dramas being played out by ants and leatherjackets, worms and tadpoles, birds and bees. It's accurate to say I became truly obsessed, and rapidly the space afforded to me in my parents' garden was no longer enough for the grand plans forming in my head. And so it was that I got my first allotment at the age of twenty-three, a sprawling overgrown plot on the outskirts of London. In my twenties I moved house half a dozen times, but wherever I was I would make the pilgrimage to my allotment, to battle weeds and grow food, and every spring there would be new grand plans. Always comfortable with verging on the eccentric, I kept the key on a string around my neck and would tell anyone who would listen all about growing food. In the office I was caught on more than one occasion shopping online for seeds when I was supposed to be working.

As I've grown older, my single-minded obsession with growing food has broadened into a greater appreciation of all plants, and these days a new flower opening its petals in my garden – bringing with it pale pinks, or yellows, bright orange, deep purple, heady scents and hoverflies – elicits a childlike joy in me. Perhaps my favourite thing of all is watching my little mistakes and oversights tell their own story: whether it's a 'weed' I've left untouched blooming into a lacy white umbellifer, or the seeds fallen from my bird-feeders erupting into bright yellow rapeseed alive with bees. For me growing food was just the gateway to what I now know will be a lifelong relationship with gardening.

In spite of how much I love it, I understand what it's like to not always have time to garden. To feel overwhelmed by the seasons, to fall behind, to neglect plants and find your plot overgrown with weeds and eaten to bits. Gardening is my passion, not my job, and like all things we *choose* to do, it often has to make way for the many other things we *have* to do. Two years ago I was finally lucky enough to get my own little garden in London. In it I grow food, of course, but I also wanted a place for nature, to grow flowers, to have space to sit and enjoy it all, somewhere to be a playground for projects, a living lab for my many experiments. It was also important for me that my garden was a place that had a quiet life of its own, that it could – up to a point – look after itself when I was too busy, and greet me with new surprises when I came back to be with it again. A sort of tag team between me and nature.

Gardening can feel like a huge and overwhelming topic full of rules and sometimes contradictory information about how to do things. I am very much of the 'get stuck in and give it a go' school of thought, and after years of trying things out, these are some of my favourite projects. Other people may do them differently, and in time you may come to find your own way of doing things. So think of this as something simple to get you started. A recipe book for having fun and making the most of your garden, patio or balcony. Just like any cookbook, you don't have to make every recipe, nor may you have the option to in your space. Instead, you can flick through and find something that catches your eye. It's enough to do just one thing, or two things, or as many as you feel inclined to, and over time you can change the recipes, swap the ingredients and make the projects your own.

THE GARDENS I HAVE LOVED

This book is full of projects as a starting point for creating your own garden, be that a balcony, a terrace, a little urban backyard or something larger. I believe starting small can lead to big things and allow you to create a garden that you will love and cherish, possibly for many years to come. So first I want to set the scene with two gardens that are dear to my heart. The first, my mum's, has evolved over many decades; the second, my own, for just a fraction of that.

My mum's garden

My parents moved into their house in London over forty years ago and my mum has been creating her own urban garden there ever since. She is originally from New Zealand and arrived here on her own at seventeen, having sailed on a ship across the world. When I finally made my own visit to her birthplace, the landscape I found allowed me to make sense of my mother's approach to gardening. New Zealand is abundant, green, wild, full of ferns, mountains, moors, damp mossy forests, huge lakes. Nature there is beautiful and powerful and always around you.

Take my mum to any garden full of plants and she'll tell you all their names. She knows how they grow and what they need, and has an eye for colour and shape, what to put where and with what. Her garden is truly one of the most beautiful I think I've ever seen. It's the kind of garden I dream of having one day. One that has lived the chapters of my life with me, rich with memories and full of plants that I have seen through many seasons.

The garden is long and narrow, divided into a series of 'rooms': a deck, beds of wildflowers, a patio, and – at the end of the garden – a shed, a magnolia, a 10-metre silver birch, and a tall hedge of laurel. Every fence is heaving with foliage and flowers, clematis, climbing roses, grape vines. What used to be a small lawn dissected with a path is now two riotous beds of wildflowers alive with bees, butterflies, even the odd hummingbird moth.

Mum always likes to remind me that on the day my brother Jack was born (he's just turned forty this year) she drove to Kent, bought a tree, planted it in the garden and then went into labour. That ornamental cherry sits in the partial shade of a silver birch. Both have roses clambering up them which are metres high and which burst into life each June with cascades of white and bright, rich pink. She has a wisteria just as old, which has reached the very top of the house. If you were to lift a plank on the deck outside the back door you'd find metres of sprawling roots running across an old patio, gnarled and thick, supporting the majestic plant above.

Bird-feeders now hang from the cherry tree she planted all those decades ago, and over a cup of tea my mum will point out the birds and tell me about their characters. She tells me what time they come to visit, that she's called the big green parakeet Peter, that the goldfinches are the messiest eaters and that she hasn't seen as many blue tits this year.

Of course, not everyone has the privilege to have a garden like this, but there are lessons here for even the smallest garden, about filling it with plants, dividing up your space, making a home for wildlife and engaging in a relationship with your garden that might just change your life.

My garden

Over the last decade I've rented across London, in places with gardens and places without, and always made the trek to my allotment to get my hands in the soil. Two years ago I bought a flat with an old friend of mine. The one thing I was adamant on was that we had to have a garden. After a year of looking we found it: the lower maisonette in a block, with a

AN INTRODUCTION

south-west-facing garden 5 metres wide and 8 metres long, one-third patio, two-thirds overgrown, lumpy lawn, and with a border already planted with Japanese anemones and a large climbing rose.

Now that I look at what my garden has become less than two years later, I see the influence of my mum's garden paired with my own tendency for excess and my long-held love of growing food. Like her I want to be surrounded by plants. I want them clambering up fences and bursting out of beds, I want different colours and textures and plenty of green. Even on this little scale, dividing up my garden into its own sections (albeit more modest than my mum's) has given me a way to navigate the space and decide what belongs where.

One of the first things I did was remove the lawn. I replaced it with a large central rectangle of gravel – underlaid with hessian rather than black plastic so that I could easily plant things through it when the fancy took me. I left an L-shaped border a metre and a half wide around the edge – the sunny section along the fence for my veg beds. The shadier end was designated as a section for wildlife. The border already being planted with perennial flowers, I kept it largely as it was, putting in spring bulbs of tulips, daffodils and alliums, sprinkling poppy seeds and willy-nilly adding gradually more plants that I'd bring home from the garden centre.

I added an archway to my gravel patio and grew sweet peas on one side and climbing beans on the other. This yielded fresh bunches of beautifully scented flowers on my desk all summer. The beans needed picking every day, there were so many. The paved patio is packed with pots, every one a little experiment containing things like potatoes, cucumbers, chillies, sweet potatoes, mint. A fig tree, a lemon tree. There's a table and chairs so that when my friends come over we can sit and have a cup of sweet lemon leaf and mint tea, or a gin and tonic full of cucumber and borage flowers. The wildlife area has a pond and a host of birds come to the feeder. I often take a chair to sit and watch all the insects that come to visit the self-sown rapeseed and sunflowers and the intentionally added chamomile, calendula and foxgloves.

In the height of summer my vegetable beds are bursting with food: courgettes, tomatoes, aubergines, kale, broccoli, chard, beetroot, garlic, tree cabbage, herbs. The beds take up just a small portion of my garden, but when in full swing it's hard to keep up with how much they produce.

As my second year has rolled around I've added more and more flowers, in pots, hanging baskets and window boxes. I've planted a much-loved pear tree directly in the ground and surrounded it with wild strawberries. I cleared a corner of my garden for something I have wanted for many years, a little greenhouse, which is now laden with cucumbers, big fat tomatoes and an array of chillies.

My garden is a beautiful jungle, but really it's a series of individual projects that you too can bring into life in your own garden.

GIVE IT A GROW

This book contains information about growing plants and plenty of projects to get you started, but most importantly, I want to encourage an approach. People so often say to me that they are overwhelmed and don't know where to start, and especially that they are worried about getting it wrong. I think starting to garden for the first time is a bit like stepping into a kitchen if you've never cooked before. We are surrounded by plants, we eat plants all the time, and just like someone who has spent their life eating but has never cooked, we may not have all the information, but that doesn't mean we don't know anything. You probably have more knowledge than you think, by simply existing in the world, and the more you learn

AN INTRODUCTION

about gardening the more it should slot into the experience you already have. For example, many plants are best started in spring, but then you probably already knew that if you thought about it, because you have lived many springs and watched the cycle of seasons come and go, and plants emerge, flower, fruit and die back.

KEY THINGS ABOUT GIVING IT A GROW

1. **You do not need to know anything to start gardening.** Just like someone who has never cooked a meal, you only need a recipe to make your first dish. You don't need to know everything about food, or indeed anything about food, to read a recipe and make a pancake. And once you've made a pancake a few times you might have learned something about cooking along the way that will help you with your next recipe.

2. **Don't be afraid to get things wrong.** Even the most seasoned gardener will tell you that things don't always go to plan in a garden. You can do the same thing year after year and the outcome will not always be the same – nature has its own ideas. One year it might be freezing cold and bone dry in winter, another mild and damp, one summer might be warm and sunny, the next dreary. One year plants will have no pests, the next they will be riddled, different bugs on different plants in different years. Gardening is about a dynamic relationship with nature – that is part of the joy, to notice and learn and have different successes in different years. To this day

I have never grown such stunning fennel bulbs as I did the first year I tried; after reading that they were hard to grow I was baffled to find them so easy, and only after many more less successful attempts did I realize I had just struck lucky.

3. **Take joy in the process.** Yes, sometimes growing your own food will save you money, but if you want an aubergine, it's almost certainly cheaper and easier to go to the shops and buy one than it is to grow one. Many people start gardening because they like the idea of picking their own food or having a pretty garden to sit in, only to find that the process, spending time outside, having projects, observing nature, building things, watching the life cycle of a plant unfold, brings them huge satisfaction, improved mental health and joy well beyond a harvest or a pretty flower.

4. **If you don't start, it won't grow.** When I have a few minutes to spare in spring or summer I often bung some seeds into a tray, knowing I could easily put it off but that the future me will be grateful to have seedlings, even those hurriedly sown where only half of them come up. When I need plants to fill the gaps in my garden, there they will be, ready to go, because I started them a few weeks before. If I spot a plant I want to take cuttings of, or I find I have an empty pot, I usually just seize the moment without a lot of thought and plant something. Seasons can move quickly in a garden, so if you have a moment just get something started.

2

THE BASICS

*No space is too small and you
don't have to do it all at once*

Even if you only have a small balcony it's possible for you to create a little oasis for nature, food and flowers. Just a tray of salad, a pot of pollinator-friendly edible flowers and a little bee drinking station or bird-feeder will make all the difference. I have often dreamed of what I might do with a big garden, but there are many benefits to smaller spaces. They are more manageable – they allow us to come up with imaginative solutions that offer great satisfaction. A small garden with a little time and care can become the Swiss army knife of the garden world, a bit of everything you want and need in a convenient little package.

Remember also that you don't have to get things laid out exactly right from the beginning – gardens evolve. The first year you might want to take time to observe any plants that are already there, to notice the way the sun moves across the space, to plant a few pots or a few plants and to plan where you want your seating area or where you might have a barbecue. After a bit of time in the space you might look at a tree in a big pot that hasn't fared so well and decide to plant it in the ground, to change the size of your garden table, get some shelves to put plants on, grow a grape vine for shade.

I say this knowing full well that I am an impatient person, and I rushed to get my garden 'done', but two years later I am grateful to realize that it's not 'finished', and as I continue to make adjustments I do it with a greater understanding of the space. In spring when I'm eyeing up a bare bit of soil, I now know in mid-summer that exact same spot will be engulfed with honeysuckle and a multitude of leaves from a Japanese anemone, and when I planned my patio this year I knew to make sure my pots had saucers to help me keep them watered in the fierce heat of the summer sun in my little garden.

TOOLS

You don't need lots of fancy kit to garden. When I plant in pots and containers I rarely use any tools at all. At its very simplest, it is possible to garden with just your hands, although it is probably sensible to wear gloves. I don't have a shed packed with kit. Just a fork and a trowel, a pair of secateurs, a hand hoe to cut down the weeds, some bamboo canes, twine for tying things, and a spade to shovel compost around. Beyond that there is very little else I use in my garden.

Trowel: Trowels are really useful for digging holes to pop plants into, as well as for scooping potting mix out of bags.

Hand fork: Especially useful for digging out stubborn long-rooted weeds.

Spade: Only useful if you have soil to dig in. Essential for putting in a pond, planting a fruit free, or shovelling homemade compost.

Secateurs: Used for pruning back plants like tomatoes, roses, grape vines and fruit trees. Ideally give them a good clean between uses to prevent the spread of disease, although I cannot promise I always remember to do this . . .

Hoe: Makes weeding very easy and leaves your soil undisturbed. You simply draw it across the surface of the soil, cutting down any small weed seedlings around your plants. A hoe can either be short- or long-handled. A long-handled one means you don't have to bend over the weed.

Twine: Try to get natural fibre twine made of jute – this is biodegradable and perfect for tying your plants to supports and securing supports together.

Bamboo canes: Useful for making supports, from single canes for plants like tomatoes to multi-cane structures like tepees for beans and cucumbers. They are also good when cut into shorter lengths for staking plants such as aubergines and broccoli and to stick in your beds to keep cats and foxes off!

PLANNING YOUR LAYOUT

To get the most out of my garden I've packed in a little bit of everything. Here are some things to consider including in your garden.

Patio: I have two areas in my garden which I consider to be patios. One is paved and home to lots of my pots and a seating area. The second is gravelled and is perfect for setting up a sun lounger or getting out the big garden table for a summer dinner party. The other benefit of the gravel is that it sits on top of soil, so I can also plant through it. My gravel patio has an archway planted either side with lavender and herbs, and each year I grow sweet peas and beans up the arch. I also plant bulbs in the corners so that I can get a seasonal display of alliums and gladioli. Both areas create open space to work in and enjoy the garden as well as to house my many pots and containers.

Seating: Gardens are there to be enjoyed! Remember not to pack so much in that you can't find a space to sit and read, drink a cup of tea, enjoy a few summer rays on your face or have a barbecue with your friends. I find a small table very useful in a little garden. Just big enough for a few cups of tea or a couple of cold glasses of rosé and some olives on a sunny Friday evening, or to have lunch at in the middle of a day working from home. I also strategically left a little gap between my greenhouse and fence so that I can keep a larger table folded away, to bring out when we have guests or if I need to pot up 100 tomatoes that I've zealously oversown.

Flower beds: I don't think there needs to be a strict divide between food and flowers – my flower bed has a pear tree and wild strawberries in it, and in my veg bed there is a climbing jasmine. But the benefit of a flower bed is that you can plan for more long-term perennial plants, like honeysuckle, roses and Japanese anemones, as well as packing it with spring bulbs. The flower bed is left mostly undisturbed and puts on a different display each season, whereas the veg beds are on a constant rotation.

Veg patch: Food plants generally like plenty of sun and rich soil, so designating an area for them can help you plan your plants across the year and give them the pampering they need. Putting this next to a fence, if it doesn't block the sun, can also give you extra vertical space to grow climbing and trailing veg such as beans, cucumbers and tomatoes. Veg beds are also good for larger plants that do best in open ground, where they can spread out their roots and need less watering than container plants.

Wildlife area: I like to think my whole garden is a wildlife area, but I still have a corner that I like to be a little wilder than the rest and in which I have put my wildlife pond and log pile, as well as wildlife-friendly plants, which often include quite a few weeds! Having a spot that is not going to be disturbed by digging and clearing helps wildlife to really settle in.

THE BASICS

A shed: This definitely isn't essential, especially if you have a small space already, but as an experimental gardener with a million projects always on the go, I find I accumulate a lot of bits and bobs and it's useful to have somewhere to keep them out of the weather. When I moved in there was a shed here already, nothing fancy, 1.2 × 1.8 metres. I would love to say it stays meticulously organized, but in reality it is either so full you can't get in, or has had a massive clean and is still very full but at least quite orderly. It's currently tidy, and I'm aiming to keep it that way. When it's tidy and organized, having a shed with your tools, pots, compost and seed trays in easy reach makes finding the things you need much simpler!

A compost area: Composting is a great way to reduce waste going to landfill at the same time as making precious nutrient-rich organic material for your garden. In my own little garden I have an area called compost corner, home to a compost bin and a wormery. I tucked it in a shady spot next to the shed where not much else was growing – in reality a bit more light wouldn't be a bad thing for the compost, but a small garden is often one with compromises. Composting is a strangely addictive and satisfying pastime. I come to see new value in cardboard, which I now hoard for a range of garden uses, not least for putting in my compost bin. See how to create your own compost on page 38.

A water source: Watering is especially important in gardens with lots of containers, as these can easily dry out. If you're like me and don't have a garden tap, you can install a water butt, which is essentially a big barrel for collecting water, with a lid to prevent evaporation and stop debris getting in. I have one near the back door that I can fill up with a hose from the kitchen tap, and another connected to the gutter on the roof of my greenhouse for collecting rainwater. Some garden tasks are best done with rainwater if you are able to collect it, such as filling up a wildlife pond or watering blueberries and other acid-loving plants, as it tends to be slightly more acidic than tap water.

A lawn: If you have the space and are up for the maintenance, then a lawn may be for you. It's a labour of love, but many gardeners wouldn't be without one. When I moved in, the middle of my garden was a lumpy, weedy lawn, which I am happy to have replaced with other things. If you do have a lawn, consider mowing less, especially during 'No-Mow May', when many wildflowers are in bloom.

A greenhouse, polytunnel, cold frame or mini greenhouse: A greenhouse is a luxury which I have gardened without for over a decade, getting my first ever proper greenhouse this year, but I have used many cheaper alternatives over the years. Covered growing areas are an extremely useful addition to a garden, providing a more stable, warm and humid environment free of cold drying wind. In the spring, they are the perfect space for starting off seedlings and acclimatizing indoor-germinated plants to the outdoors. In the summer they allow you to grow heat-loving plants that wouldn't do well outside, and you can grow fresh salad leaves throughout the winter. For years I have used small movable cold frames (page 116). These are little clear boxes with a lid and no base which I can pop straight on top of my veg beds and which give me lush early salad leaves, spinach and radishes in the spring and salad leaves through the winter. Inexpensive PVC greenhouses are widely available and easily assembled, offering a budget-friendly option for starting seeds in spring, hardening off plants or growing one or two potted cucumbers, melons or tomatoes in the summer. However, they don't last very long and are not the most sustainable option.

Sunlight and shade

The first thing I consider when laying out a garden is sunlight. The aspect (the direction your garden faces) determines which areas are going to be in shade and which are in full sunlight. Sunlight is a precious resource in a garden and will dictate what you can grow and where. Poor soil, a concrete patio, wet ground, can all be overcome, but sunlight can rarely be amended, which means it's an important thing to take into consideration when planning the layout of your garden.

- Put vegetable beds or pots of edible plants in the sunniest spot in your garden, prioritizing fruiting vegetables, as these require the most sun (tomatoes, beans, cucumbers, courgettes, chillies, etc. all love lots of sun!), and anything that naturally comes from sunny hot places, such as Mediterranean herbs.

- Annual, fast-growing flowers will also benefit from a sunny spot in your garden, for example zinnias, marigolds, cosmos and sunflowers, all of which love plenty of sun to give their best performance.

- Utilize spots with slightly less sunlight by growing edible plants like leafy greens, which have lower light needs and benefit from cooler, shady parts of the garden in summer. Lettuce, spinach, mustard greens, coriander, mint, parsley, chard, kale and rocket are all great options.

- Shadier areas are a good place to put a garden shed and to grow lots of lush green shade-tolerant plants. Plants native to woodland habitats, such as ferns, ivy and foxgloves, are great for shady spots, so why not turn a darker corner into a wildlife area and add a log pile?

- Spend time observing your space at different times of day, making a mental note (or take photos!) of where gets the sun first, which spots get the sun for the longest, and which areas get the most intense sunlight in the middle of the day. Bear in mind, spots in shade during the winter (when the sun is low) are likely to get more sun during the summer months when the sun is higher.

- Think about where you want to sit and enjoy your garden – do you prefer to lounge in the sun, or shelter in the shade in the middle of summer? Plants are important, but so is having space to sit and enjoy your garden!

GROWING IN POTS AND CONTAINERS

You don't need a lot of space to start a garden. Many of us, especially in cities, have an outdoor space that has no open ground, such as a patio or a balcony, or maybe we rent and either aren't allowed to plant things in the garden or don't want to leave plants behind when we leave. These are all good reasons to grow things in pots and containers, and many plants thrive in them.

How to fill your pots

For many of us the easiest way to get potting mix for our pots and containers is to buy it in bags from the garden centre, although you can also have a go at making your own. The choice can be a little overwhelming, but there are essentially two main types of compost you would use in a pot or container:

Multipurpose compost: The most widely available compost, often for sale outside large supermarkets in the growing season.

THE BASICS

Historically made with peat, this is now substituted with a range of materials such as composted bark, coconut coir, wood fibres and even wool, and also usually contains some plant food. Multipurpose compost is suitable for growing a wide variety of short-lived annual plants and vegetables. It does tend to dry out quickly and then is difficult to rehydrate, so you need to be vigilant with watering. The nutrients in the compost can deplete quickly, meaning it's usually recommended to use a liquid feed on plants in pots and containers after the first few weeks.

Soil-based compost: Often labelled as John Innes, this compost is different from multipurpose compost because it contains soil, which is combined with a peat substitute (such as those mentioned above), as well as sand and plant food. The advantage of soil-based compost is that it holds on to nutrients longer, dries out more slowly and is heavier, so provides more stability for mature and taller plants. John Innes comes in various types, including seed compost and Nos. 1, 2 and 3. These numbers refer to the varying levels of fertilizer in the mix, with 3 containing the most nutrients and being the most suitable for mature, long-lived potted plants. Soil-based compost is especially well suited for potting up fruit trees and shrubs, or anything tall like beans that need a more stable base.

Additions: There are also several products available that you can add to your potting mixes. These are the ones I use most:

- **Coconut coir:** Made from the husks of coconuts, coir is commonly used in peat-free compost mixes, and can be bought in compressed blocks which you hydrate. It holds moisture well, has a nice fine texture that's good for starting seeds and is a lot easier to carry home than a bag of compost! It can easily be bought online and is a good way to bulk out mixes for large pots and containers.

- **Perlite:** This is a kind of white expanded volcanic rock that looks a bit like polystyrene. Adding a handful or two to seed starting mixes or pots can improve drainage and aeration to plant roots. It's especially useful for any plants that love very free-draining soil.

- **Vermiculite:** A mineral that has been expanded under intense heat to produce fine flakes, this can be added like perlite to mixes to aid drainage, but it also retains water so it can help keep potting mix moist. It's especially useful for covering freshly sown seeds that don't like being buried too deeply.

- **Grit:** Like perlite, grit is added to potting mix to improve drainage.

Make your own potting mix: If you have access to garden soil and organic matter such as homemade compost (see page 38) or leaf mould, then it's possible to have a go at making your own potting mix. Simply combine two parts garden soil with one part homemade compost, to make a mix that's suitable for trees, fruit and crops like potatoes. Adding some drainage material such as grit will help prevent the mix getting too compacted. Bear in mind that shop-bought potting mix is sterile, which means it doesn't have weed seeds in, whereas homemade mixes may sprout a lot of weeds. Making your own mix will of course have variable results, depending on the soil in your garden and the quality of your homemade compost, but I like the idea of using as much of what I have as possible and experimenting. I've grown potatoes very successfully in containers using just garden soil and a little organic plant food.

Drainage

Plant roots need oxygen, which they absorb from the air spaces between soil particles. This means it's really important to make sure any excess water can easily drain out of your pots and containers, as waterlogged pots risk literally suffocating the roots of your plants.

- **Drainage holes:** Any container you use for growing in needs drainage holes in the bottom for excess water to escape. Most pots come with good drainage holes, but if you are upcycling a bucket or other container then you will need to make some. The easiest way to do this is to use an electric drill with a suitable drill bit. Ideally you want holes about 1cm or more across – tiny holes are more likely to get blocked by soil and roots. Some hanging basket liners also don't have holes, so make sure to check and make them with a pair of scissors if necessary.

- **Drainage material:** It's a good idea to put drainage material such as broken bits of pot or a small handful of gravel in the bottom of your pot or container to stop holes getting blocked by soil and roots and so ensure that water can easily flow out.

- **Raise pots off the ground:** You can improve drainage by raising your pots off the ground so that the drainage holes aren't pressed against a hard, flat surface, which makes the water slower to drain off. You can buy little terracotta feet to stand your pots on, or put them on some garden shelving.

- **Add drainage to the soil:** Mixing grit or perlite into your potting mix will allow liquid to drain through your potting mix more quickly, making it less likely to stay too wet. Both these materials also have the benefit of creating extra air holes in your soil mix, which will keep the oxygen flowing to your plant's roots.

Watering

One of the biggest issues with growing in pots is getting the moisture level right. Here are a few top tips for keeping your pots hydrated. If your pots get very dry, it can be difficult to rehydrate them again. The water instead runs straight out of the bottom of the pot, leaving you thinking you've watered, only to find when scraping back the top of the soil that it's still bone dry.

- **A soaking station:** The best way to rehydrate very dry pots is to sit them in water. I have a large metal tub in my garden that I keep partially filled with water, but any container large enough to sit a big pot or several small ones in would work. When I spot a sad drooping plant, I just pop it in there and leave it until it's sprung back to life.

- **Plant saucers:** Plant saucers are a great way to catch the water that runs straight through a pot and out the bottom, holding it in the saucer so the soil can gradually soak it up. Ideally your plant saucers will be empty an hour after watering – if they are still full, pour away the excess water so your pots aren't too wet. Plant saucers come in a range of sizes for different pots, or you can even use old dinner plates.

- **Re-use bottles:** This is such a useful little hack and a great way to re-use plastic bottles or wine bottles. Fill up a clean wine bottle with water, then turn the bottle upside down and quickly push the neck into your pot. This works best when there is something like a wall or another pot to lean the bottle on, or you can pop a bamboo cane next to it and tie the bottle to it, to make it more secure. The water will gradually flow out of the bottle, allowing the soil to slowly soak it up. For even slower watering (for example, if you are going on holiday), you can make three or four holes in the lid of a plastic water bottle, fill the bottle with water, screw on the lid and bury the neck upside down in the pot. It will drip out even more slowly over several days.

- **Mulch:** Mulching means applying a layer to the surface of the soil. It has several benefits, including reducing water loss to evaporation and suppressing weeds. There are lots of different mulches you can add to the top of your pots, like bark chips and straw. You can also use more decorative mulches such as grit or gravel, pebbles, shells, or even tumbled glass.

- **Drip irrigation:** If you have a lot of pots, find it hard to keep on top of watering or find that you are regularly away, then installing a drip irrigation system may be worthwhile. The device is connected to a garden tap, then you run a pipe to each of your pots. Set on a timer, the water comes on automatically for an allotted time and slowly hydrates your pots. Something I would probably use if I had a garden tap!

Can you re-use compost?

This is a question I get asked all the time, and the answer is absolutely. Shop-bought compost is expensive, and I wouldn't dream of using it for a single season and throwing it out. Here are some of the ways you can use it in the garden.

- **Revive it for use in containers**: After being used for the first time, your compost will likely be full of roots and depleted of nutrients. Tip it out and break it up, removing old roots, then add some new organic material such as shop-bought or your own homemade compost (page 38). Use about a quarter new organic material to three-quarters old compost. I also add a little sprinkle of slow-release organic plant food according to the application instructions on the packet, then it's ready to use.

- **Use it to top up veg beds:** During the autumn and winter, I top up my veg beds with a new layer of organic matter, to be slowly incorporated into the soil ready for planting next spring. Old compost is a great thing to use for this – just tip it out and spread it.

- **Mulch your plants:** You can re-use compost on other existing beds around established plants like fruit trees and roses, or over herbaceous perennials that you want to protect over the winter.

GROW VERTICALLY

We're used to thinking of the size of our garden in terms of how many metres wide and long it is, but to think of just the footprint of a garden overlooks a whole swathe of prime gardening real estate. Whether it's using an archway, a window box or growing plants up your fence, growing 'up' gives you loads of extra space. Not only that, but particularly in a small garden it creates the feeling of an enclosed oasis. I love to be literally surrounded by plants, and growing vertically is the best way to do it.

Containers: Hanging baskets and window boxes, or little pots with hooks, are a great way to create more growing space in your garden. Try putting up hanging basket brackets on exterior walls or at the top of sturdy fence posts. Raised containers like this allow you to make the most of the sunniest spots in the garden, because they are high up and less likely to be overshadowed. Window boxes with hooks are also a great way to use railings or sturdy fences.

Archways: I'm a big fan of archways, which are an extremely efficient use of space while also creating a wonderful lush height in your garden. Walking through an archway covered in flowers and food is a summer highlight. I like to plant sweet peas and climbing beans on mine, but clematis, or the beautiful exotic *Mina lobata*, would also be stunning. As for food, there's loads of options, from cucumbers and indeterminate cherry tomatoes, to grape vines and tall summer-fruiting raspberries.

Tepees: These are attractive and easy to put together, and great for growing sweet peas, mangetout, runner beans and climbing French beans. They could also be used to train sweet potato vines or to grow cucumbers. For a simple structure to use for one season, use long bamboo canes. Push the canes securely into the soil (or a pot) in a circle, spacing them about a foot apart – you can do this with just three canes or up to about ten. Bring the tops of the canes together so they are crossing each other, then tie securely with twine around the point where they cross.

Shelves: I have lots of shelves in my garden, which add attractive levels and help to keep things organized. My masses of pots and seed trays look a lot better on my tiered shelves than they would all laid out across my patio. A mini greenhouse with several shelves also creates space for lots of trays and pots of seedlings while taking up just a small footprint.

HOW TO START SEEDS

Growing your own plants from seed is extremely satisfying and it's also a lot cheaper than buying plants. Getting out the seed box in late winter marks the start of a new year in the garden for me. A single packet of lettuce seeds can have hundreds, if not thousands, of seeds in it! A thing to bear in mind – most seeds are a bit like Goldilocks, they like conditions to be 'just right'. All gardeners have had seeds that don't come up, so here are a few tips to get them off to a good start.

Indoors or outdoors?

Some seeds are best sown indoors and others outside. The main deciding factor is usually whether plants can cope with the cold.

What to sow indoors
- Tender plants that need a long growing season. This includes things like chillies, aubergines and tomatoes. These plants won't have enough time to mature if you wait until it's warm enough to start them outside.
- Tender plants that you want to give a head start for earlier fruits or flowers in the garden. Veg like beans, courgettes and cucumbers, and flowers like cosmos and zinnias, can be sown outside when it warms up, but you may want to start them indoors for an earlier result.

What to sow outdoors

- Hardy seeds can be started outside when it's still fairly cool, for example spinach, lettuce, spring onions and brassicas, but early sowings will benefit from the protection of a greenhouse, cold frame or even a plastic propagator lid over an individual tray.

- As it warms up, they can be sown without protection in trays or pots outside or directly in the ground.

- After the risk of frost has passed, and the weather has warmed up, tender plants like beans and courgettes can be sown outside, where they often benefit from plenty of natural light. I still start them in pots or trays before planting them out in their final location.

- Root crops like carrots are best sown directly where they are going to grow, as they don't like their roots being disturbed.

- Hardy annual flowers like calendula, borage and poppies.

What containers to start seeds in:

There are lots of different ways you can sow seeds, depending on what you have:

Module trays: Module trays are really useful for growing little plug plants that can then be popped out into the garden. It means you can start your next crop before your first one is finished, and the little plants are often better able to cope with pests than seeds sown direct. It's worth investing in quality solid recycled plastic modules, as many of the cheaper ones will disintegrate after a couple of years.

Seed trays: Seed trays are oblong trays with drainage holes that you can use to sow seedlings densely. You can sow a whole tray with one variety of seed or do rows that you can label. Once the seeds germinate and have grown their first few leaves, they will need 'pricking out' (see page 35).

Pots: Pots are good for sowing larger seeds like courgettes and cucumbers, or for potting up small seedlings that need longer to grow before going outside (like tomatoes).

Soil blocks: A soil blocker is a device that allows you to turn a wet compost mix into cubes that hold together without a pot or tray. The device is expensive but can be used for many years, and is a good option for those wanting to avoid plastic.

Recycling containers from your kitchen: You don't need specially made seed trays to start seeds. I often use the trays that tomatoes and mushrooms from the supermarket come in, to sow seeds. If they don't already have drainage holes you can easily make some, and use them as you would a normal seed tray.

- There are also lots of uses for plastic takeaway boxes. For example, you can use them to test out older seeds by germinating them before planting. Just wrap the seeds in wet tissue and pop them into a box, then plant only those that germinate. I also find these boxes perfect for keeping my smallest seed blocks moist after planting. I even make a little cutout flap in the top so I can control the moisture levels inside the box.

- Egg boxes are useful for chitting potatoes (more on that in the potato section, page 141) and can also be used to sow seeds – although be careful, as they can easily dry out.

THE BASICS

What potting mix to use

- The simplest way to start seeds is to use a shop-bought compost mix. There are plenty of seed-specific composts available, but I find multipurpose compost with any large pieces removed works fine.

- Coconut coir is an alternative for sowing seeds, and you can often buy small discs which expand when soaked in water and can be planted into directly.

- Adding perlite to your compost can help improve aeration and drainage.

- Vermiculite is useful for covering seeds that do not like to be buried too deeply, like tomatoes, poppies and strawberries, and can be added to soil mixes to improve moisture retention.

How to sow them

- Different seeds have different sowing requirements, but luckily most seed packets come with instructions on when to sow them. If not, there are many great guides online, for example the Royal Horticultural Society website.

- It's best to follow the instructions for the correct time of year to start your seeds, as this has been worked out based on how long the plants need to flower or fruit and the conditions they need to grow in. But there is always a little leeway for experimenting.

- Fill your chosen container with your seed compost and sow the seeds at the specified depth.

Keep your seeds moist

Keeping seeds and seedlings moist, but not wet, is essential to successful germination. Too wet, they can rot, too dry and they will either fail to germinate or seedlings will quickly die.

- After sowing your seeds, make sure you water them. To prevent your seeds being disturbed, you can sit your sown pots or trays in water until they are damp all the way to the surface. Alternatively, water them from the top with a fine rose attachment on a watering can, but bear in mind that this may wash small seeds around, which may cause confusion if you've sown different seeds in the same tray. Allow any excess water to drain off, so that your compost is not waterlogged.

- After sowing, to keep your soil damp but not wet, the best thing to do is cover it to create a consistent stable environment.

- Propagators: These handy bits of kit consist of a tray with a plastic dome lid. After sowing you can put your pots or seed trays inside a propagator to stop them drying out. Because the base tray has no holes in it, it also means water and soil won't escape on to your windowsill, and once your seedlings come up it's easier to water them.

- If you don't have a propagator, you can improvise by popping pots or trays inside a large ziplock bag, inside a Tupperware, or covering with a sheet of glass or Perspex. Leave a little gap for airflow. Seeds sown indoors are especially susceptible to drying out.

Some like it hot

Different seeds need different temperatures to germinate.

- For most seeds started indoors a sunny windowsill is warm enough, but you will get quicker and often better germination if you can give certain seeds an extra boost. You can get heated propagators or heat mats to go underneath your seeds and give out a gentle heat that keeps them at a snug 20°C. There is a wide range on the market, but you can pick one up for around £20 to £30 and they can be used for many years. They are especially useful for germinating heat-loving plants such as melons, cucumbers, chillies, tomatoes, beans and sweetcorn.

Give them light

Once seeds come up they will start seeking light immediately. Without enough light their little stems tend to stretch out and become leggy and weak.

- Light intensity increases from the shortest day, so is weakest in mid-winter, when the days are not only short but the light itself is low on power. So if you only have a windowsill to start off seedlings, it pays to wait a couple of months until early to mid-spring and start sowing when the light is stronger.

- If you are desperate to start seeds super early, it's best to use a grow-light. While there are a huge range of lights available, some very expensive, I've got a couple of LED panel lights that I picked up for about £25 each which have always done the job.

Potting up

If you start lots of seedlings in a tray together or in small modules, they may need transferring to a larger pot before they are ready for their final spot in the garden. This is especially common with tomatoes, which spend quite a long time growing indoors before they go out and often outgrow their original container.

Hardening off

Now this is a hurdle at which many new gardeners fall, a step that, if you are impatient like me, you want to just skip because it's a faff. But in this case, it's a faff that's worth it. Your little indoor plants have spent their whole lives in a nice warm house – no cold nights, no wind, no blazing hot sun. If you turf them out into your garden the shock might literally kill them. They can collapse if left out on a cold night, and in the daytime their leaves can get burnt by the sun. So you need to adjust them gradually.

- When all risk of frost has passed and when it's not raining or blowing a gale, put your plants outside for the day, out of direct sunlight. At night bring them back in. If you have lots of plants, the easiest way to do this is to put them on trays so you can easily take them in and out in just a few batches.

- After a few days of this, leave them out overnight but with some protection – in a cold frame or mini greenhouse if you have one, or under a table or bench with a blanket thrown over.

- Do this for a few more nights and your plants should be acclimatized. Now you can plant them out in your garden.

GARDENING JARGON

Lots of gardening instructions are written with the assumption of prior knowledge and therefore aren't always the most accessible to newbies. Here are some words that you may not be familiar with and what they mean:

Annual: This is a plant that completes its life cycle in a single year, from seed to flower, and dies the same year. Lots of vegetables are grown as annuals, such as radishes, potatoes, tomatoes, lettuces, beans and cucumbers. Annuals also include flowers such as calendulas, zinnias, cosmos, marigolds and sunflowers.

Biennial: This is a plant that completes its life cycle over two years. Many vegetables that we grow as annuals (we harvest them in the first year) actually have a two-year life cycle and if left in the ground will go on to flower the following year – this includes carrots and beetroot as well as brassicas like kales and cabbages. Flowers that you sow one year and wait until the second year to flower include foxgloves, nicotiana and hollyhocks.

Perennial: This is a plant that will live for several years. In the veg garden that's things like asparagus, globe artichokes, perennial kales, and fruit bushes. For flowers, things like roses, honeysuckle, Japanese anemones, peonies and hydrangeas. Some perennials will die down completely over the winter and return with new growth the following year, and these are known as herbaceous perennials.

Tender: A tender plant is one that is not tolerant of freezing temperatures. Frosts will kill or severely damage tender plants. This includes many vegetables and flowers that are grown as annuals, such as tomatoes, cucumbers, beans, zinnias and cosmos, as well as perennials accustomed to warmer climates, like lemongrass, citrus and dahlias.

Hardy: Plants that can survive year-round changes in the climate, including cold and frost.

Deciduous: These are trees, shrubs and perennials that lose their leaves during part of the year, usually winter, and grow new ones each spring.

Evergreen: These plants keep their leaves all year round, staying green during the winter.

Hardening off: The process of gradually acclimatizing plants that have been sown or grown indoors to outdoor conditions. Seedlings grown on a windowsill will have a shock from the bright sun, dry wind and night-time cold of the outside world, and if they are moved suddenly, they may suffer or even die. Hardening off gradually introduces them outside over a couple of weeks (more information on page 32).

Cutting: A cutting allows you to make new plants from existing ones. At its simplest, a non-flowering stem is cut from a plant, the lower leaves are removed, and it is put into a pot of damp compost to root. Rooting powder can be used to encourage roots to form, and cuttings should be covered with a sandwich bag or similar so they stay moist until they root. Cuttings can be taken in slightly different ways from different plants, and there's no harm in experimenting.

Deadheading: This is the process of removing finished flowers from ornamental plants to keep them producing new flowers for longer. Plants flower in order to produce seed, so if you remove the finished flowers the plants will often respond by producing more. It's a great way to get your sweet peas and dahlias to keep producing new blooms.

Firming in: After planting a new plant it's a good idea to gently press down around the rootball to ensure good contact with the soil and to give the plant stability.

THE BASICS

Grafting: The process of joining two different plants together to create one single plant. It's an ancient technique which is commonly used to produce fruit trees where the lower plant (rootstock) provides the roots and determines the size of the tree, and the top part (scion) is a cutting from an existing fruit tree, allowing copies to be made of a desirable variety. Grafting can also be done with food plants like aubergines, tomatoes, melons and cucumbers to make vigorous plants that can grow better in cooler conditions. This isn't a technique that many gardeners do themselves but is useful to know when buying plants.

Pinching out: Removing tender growth on a plant with your fingers. You may do this to remove the top of annual flowers like sweet peas and cosmos when the plants are small, to encourage side shoots. The tops of plants such as broad beans and tomatoes may be pinched out when they reach their required height, or you may remove side shoots on plants to limit growth to a single main stem.

Pricking out: If you sow seeds in a tray, this is the process of gently removing the seedlings once they've come up so you can plant them out or transfer them into pots of their own.

Pruning: Cutting back a plant to control its shape and promote new growth. Pruning fruit trees each year, for example, helps you to determine the plant's final shape.

Thinning: If you sow seeds directly in the ground – such as carrots – this is the process of removing some of the seedlings when they come up to make room for the others to grow.

True leaves: When seedlings first appear, the first set of leaves which unfold from the seed often don't look like the leaves of the mature plant. These first leaves are called cotyledons, and the second set of leaves, which are known as 'true leaves', reveals the actual shape of the plant's leaves.

Rootbound: When plants have spent a long time in the same pot, or seedlings have been in a very small pot a little too long, they can become what's known as rootbound. The roots spiral round inside the pot and can become quite compact. Generally, it's a good idea to loosen these roots when moving the plant to the ground or to a larger pot. But potting up regularly will reduce the chances of plants becoming rootbound and should help you avoid needing to disturb the roots, which not all plants like.

Running to seed/bolting: Plants are trying to reproduce, and for many that involves making seeds. Even lettuces and leeks, which we don't often think of as flowering plants, need to produce seed to make the next generation. In vegetable gardening we often want to harvest the plant to eat before this happens, but if we miss the window, we refer to the plant as 'bolting' or 'running to seed'. Plants such as lettuces, spinach and radishes will start to grow a tall stem and will flower. This often happens in response to changing amounts of light across a year, or if the plant gets hot and dry.

Transplanting: This is when you move a seedling or plant from one place to another. For example, moving seedlings from a module tray into their final growing position in a pot or in the ground.

HOW TO NURTURE YOUR GARDEN

Sometimes people say to me, 'I plant things and then they just die, it's very disheartening.' It's true that when things don't go to plan it can be disappointing. But there is one thing that can massively improve your chances of success. It's a simple concept.

THE BASICS

Gardening, at its simplest, is an ongoing process of nurturing. If you plant something and forget about it, it's highly likely it will die, dry out, get overgrown by weeds or be eaten by pests. Gardening is about the process of continuing to notice your plants, to make little changes to keep them happy, to think about what they need and give it to them in the form of sunlight, good soil, water and protection.

It may sound a little like a chore, but over time learning what your plants need is really the key to success and the joy of having a garden. It's possible that even when you do this your carefully laid plans may still be foiled – your cat might decide to dig up your beetroot to go to the loo, a cold snap might freeze your strawberry flowers, you might accidentally leave your cucumber seedlings in the garden on a cold night and they will collapse. It's not to say you can't ever make mistakes, or that nature might not have other plans. It's just to have the idea that plants are living, growing things that need a little attention to thrive.

Taking care of your soil

If you have soil in your garden, as opposed to a balcony or patio, a common question new gardeners have is, what sort of soil do I need? Soil is vitally important – it is the foundation of your garden and taking care of the soil is one of the best ways you can take care of your plants. Soil regulates the flow of water, nutrients and air to your plants' roots, and getting this balance right, alongside enough sunlight, is the secret to happy, healthy plants.

Garden soil is a lottery depending on where you live and how it has been used previously – some are heavy clay, some light and sandy and others somewhere in between, but most soils can benefit from improvement to make them a good home for your plants, especially edible ones. Many plants require 'fertile soil' – this is soil which is rich in organic matter and nutrients and has a structure that makes those nutrients easily available to plants, holds enough water and allows plant roots to grow easily. Less fertile soils, on the other hand, may be very dry, low in nutrients, compacted or waterlogged, making them less hospitable.

Luckily, there is one easy way to improve your soil's fertility regardless of what soil you have to start with, and that's adding organic matter. Organic matter includes things like homemade compost, well-rotted manure, leaf mould, which is essentially composted leaves, and products from the shops like multi-purpose compost and soil conditioner. Adding these materials feeds the multitude of micro-organisms living in your soil, which in turn break down the organic matter and gradually release the essential nutrients they contain. This process also improves the structure of the soil and makes it better able to regulate the moisture and nutrients available to your plants.

Organic matter like leaf mould, manure and homemade compost also provides habitats for beetles, centipedes and worms, which in turn add biodiversity to your garden and support other wildlife, such as birds. Plants grown in healthy soil rich with lots of organic matter may not need any additional feeding, which is great for the soil and your bank balance. Traditionally organic matter has been dug into new beds to prepare them for planting, but these days 'no-dig' is increasingly popular, where the organic matter is just put on top and left to be incorporated by the residents of the soil (more on page 60). I add organic matter to my beds every autumn in the form of homemade or shop-bought compost.

How to make compost

Compost is an incredible way to recycle waste and turn it into living, breathing soil for your garden. It's also a fantastic way you can personally help to combat climate change, because food waste buried at landfill is a huge source of methane, a potent greenhouse gas that is about twenty-eight times more powerful at warming the planet than carbon dioxide. Having a compost bin in your own garden means you can constantly supply it with kitchen scraps, household paper and card waste. I'm going to give a few basic principles of composting here, including what works for me in my small garden. Entry-level composting, if you will.

What to put your compost in

In a little urban garden it may seem there is not enough space to start a compost pile, but it can be done. You can compost in a large bin, create a bay using pallets, or even just mound it up on a spare patch of ground. I have also seen examples of people drilling air holes in plastic buckets and bins and using them successfully to make compost. At its most basic you can also bury compost in a hole in the garden. I just use a cone-shaped plastic compost bin that was already in the garden when I moved in.

The key ingredients

As a newbie it's a common assumption to think that kitchen veg scraps are the main ingredient in compost, but the secret is getting a balance of different kinds of materials, which will give you the best compost the most quickly.

- **Green waste and brown waste:** The most important basic principle of composting is that you need two different kinds of material:
  - Green waste gives you nitrogen and includes your kitchen vegetable scraps, coffee grounds, grass cuttings, annual weeds and any other leafy green plant material.
  - Brown waste gives you carbon and includes things like dry leaves, cardboard, paper, egg boxes, straw, chopped-up twigs and wood chips.

- For a rich, well-balanced (not sludgy or smelly) compost you need to make sure you keep adding plenty of brown alongside your green. I keep a bucket of torn-up cardboard and paper next to my compost bin so that when I add fresh scraps from the kitchen, I can always pop a layer of brown waste on top. This also makes your compost less likely to attract any unwanted visitors.

- **Air:** Composting is primarily done by micro-organisms, which need oxygen to function. There are a few ways you can add air to your compost. The most traditional is to turn it with a fork, which is more practical when you have large open bays of compost. For smaller compost bins like mine, you can use a compost aerator (a sort of spiral tool), or use a tip I picked up from the composting expert Kate Flood (@compostable.kate), which is to add a tube down the middle of your compost so air can circulate without you having to turn it. I used a PVC pipe drilled with holes, but Kate also suggests using a bundle of sticks or a tube of chicken wire.

- **Moisture**: You want your compost heap to be moist but not soggy. Usually there is quite a lot of moisture from kitchen scraps, and during the damp winter months I never have to add any water to my bin. In the summer it is worth checking on your compost and pouring over some water if it's looking a little dry.

- **Time:** How long it takes compost to be ready varies, but it's approximately a year, which does sound like a long time. I think of it as a garden bin that swallows up my kitchen, garden and cardboard scraps and every now and then gives me great compost for my garden.

When is it ready?

As a general guide your compost is ready when the majority of the material has broken down, leaving just some woody bits, and it smells earthy. If you only have a small compost set-up like me, which you continuously add to, it may not all be ready at the same time. I extract mine in autumn, by lifting the top off, removing the bottom layers which are most composted and then putting the top layers back in the bin to carry on composting. Compost can then be spread on your beds, added to potting mixes or used as a mulch around plants.

HOW TO MAKE A WORMERY

In addition to my compost bin, I have a wormery. Luckily this was fairly easy to get started, since my compost heap was already alive with composting worms – these tend to arrive and breed in bins sitting on soil with no bottom, or to which garden matter, soil and roots are added. Unlike earthworms, which are soil dwellers, composting worms are smaller and redder and can be found in decaying organic matter. If you don't have a compost bin, or a friend who has one and can give you some worms, it is possible to buy compost worms online. Find a reputable local supplier and they can send you a box of worms in the post. A wormery is great for composting in a small space, as the worms break material down faster and in the process add plenty of nutrients and beneficial microbes in the form of rich vermicompost, called castings (otherwise known as worm poo). Just like a compost bin, your wormery needs brown and green waste, but also sufficient drainage, darkness and a bit of grit.

You will need:
2 identical large containers that fit one inside the other, not transparent (worms like it dark) – make sure one container has a lid
A drill with a drill bit 0.8mm or larger
2 bricks
Bedding – such as shredded paper / leaf mould / peat-free compost /coconut coir
An organic piece of cloth such as hessian or a natural material blanket
Compost worms

1. Start by drilling plenty of holes in the bottom of your first container. These holes are to let liquid out of the bottom of your wormery (worm farms produce a liquid known as 'worm leachate'). Next, make a row of holes along each side of your container an inch or so from the top to ensure good air circulation.
2. The second container will be used to catch the liquid that the worm farm produces. (If you only have one container you can do without the second one, just place the bricks on the ground and sit your one container on top. Expect some leakage.)
3. Put one brick at either end in the bottom of the container without holes and put the container with holes inside. Thanks to the bricks, the top container will sit a few inches above the bottom one, so the holes around the top of your container are open to the air.
4. Now put 10–15cm of worm bedding inside your top container. Make sure the bedding is moist

but not soggy, and add a little water if needed – rainwater is best.
5. Once you've put in the bedding, add your worms and top with a little more bedding. If you have access to it, adding a handful of garden soil will also help to introduce beneficial bacterial and soil microbes. Then tuck them in with a blanket to keep it moist and dark, pop the lid on and place your wormery out of direct sun. Mine is in a shady part of my garden, next to a fence. But a shed is also a great place for a wormery.
6. After a few days, the worms can be fed: aim for two-thirds green waste in the form of cut-up kitchen fruit and vegetable scraps, coffee grounds, tea leaves and small amounts of chopped-up green garden waste. But avoid chillies, onions and garlic, as well as citrus peels, any animal-derived, processed or cooked foods such as meat, dairy, oils, bread or pasta. You will also need to add about one-third brown waste in the form of cardboard, dry leaves and egg boxes. Worms need a small amount of grit to help with their digestion, which can be supplied by the occasional scoop of garden soil.
7. Continue to add to your worm farm little and often. If there are lots of food scraps that haven't yet been broken down, wait a little while before adding more so the worms can catch up.
8. Check the bottom container for excess liquid and remove it – it's important your worms don't get waterlogged. Some people swear by this liquid as a great plant food, diluted with 10 parts water. It's worth noting that you should chuck it if it

smells bad, and that its nutritional composition can be variable.
9. In the winter your worms will slow down in their processing of scraps, and it's best to keep them out of extreme cold. If you can, move your bin to a shed and wrap it with layers like blankets or bubble wrap to keep warmth in.
10. When your wormery is full and the material has broken down, which will take about 8 to 12 months, you can remove your worm compost. There are a couple of ways to do this. First, as the majority of the worms are usually found in the top layer, remove this and set it aside, then remove the largely worm-free material below. Alternatively, on a sunny day spread the contents of your wormery on to a tarp, and put a layer of damp newspaper over the middle. The worms should migrate under the paper, and you can collect the worm-free castings from the outside.

Feeding your plants

The energy that plants need to grow comes from sunlight, but they still need a host of nutrients to reach their full potential. Many of these nutrients are found in soil, so plants grown in fertile ground which has been enriched with organic matter like homemade or shop-bought compost will generally need less or no feeding, while plants in pots, which have only a limited amount of soil to draw their nutrients from, can definitely benefit from a feed. The main thing to remember is that less is more when it comes to plant food. A very common mistake as a beginner gardener is to over-feed plants, thinking the more food the better. But too many nutrients can severely damage and stunt the growth of your plants, and it's not great for the environment either. So always follow the instructions on any product you buy, and above all concentrate on creating healthy soil for your plants to grow in.

What nutrients do plants need?

You'll find three main nutrients in plant food, and plants use them for different things. This is useful to know when diagnosing what your plant needs – for example, if you have a root veg that's all leaf and no root it may be due to too much nitrogen, or if your courgette has stopped flowering, it could probably do with a dose of high-potassium feed.

Nitrogen: Promotes leafy growth.

Phosphorus: Gives roots and shoots a boost.

Potassium: Helps plants flower and fruit.

Fertilizers

Fruit and vegetables are especially nutrient-hungry plants and a feed with a fertilizer will often boost growth, flowering and fruiting. Bear in mind that poor growth can be caused by many other factors, such as not enough water, not enough space to grow, or pests and diseases, rather than a lack of nutrients. So just chucking fertilizer on a struggling plant is unlikely to solve all its problems!

Fertilizers can be either synthetic or organic, and if you want to garden organically you'll need to avoid not only synthetic pesticides but synthetic fertilizers too. Organic fertilizers are made from materials like seaweed and animal waste and are my chosen option in the garden.

Liquid plant food

Liquid feeds are a good way to give plants a rapid nutrient boost, but they are easily washed away and won't stay in the soil for long. A balanced organic feed is good for a range of plants and those in initial stages of growth, and it's best to switch to a high-potassium feed for heavy-fruiting plants such as tomatoes, cucumbers, aubergines and beans every week or two once they start to flower. They are easy to use – dilute with water to the recommended concentration and pour them around the base of your plants.

Granular plant food

These break down in the soil more slowly and so are available to plants for a longer period of time, but it also means it can take time for them to start working. This includes things like: chicken manure pellets; blood, fish and bone; and other powdered or graduated organic-based plant foods. These can be added to pots when planting them up, popped into a planting hole in the ground or used to top-dress the soil in spring to help ready it for the year ahead.

Make your own plant food

If you have them to hand, comfrey and nettles are both great plants for making your own plant food, but they are often much weaker than shop-bought fertilizers. Be warned, though, the smell made in the process is not for the faint-hearted! Comfrey is high in potassium, so is especially good for feeding fruiting plants like tomatoes, peppers, cucumbers, berries and fruit trees, and nettles are high in nitrogen, which is great for leafy greens.

Comfrey tea
- To make the most concentrated comfrey tea, collect comfrey leaves using gloves, chop them up and pack the leaves tightly in a bucket, then place a brick on top and cover with a lid.

- Check the contents of your bucket every few weeks. The leaves will break down and produce a smelly brown liquid. Pour this off and store in a bottle. You can add more leaves over time.

- Your stored feed can be diluted 1 part feed to 10 parts water and watered on to your plants.

Nettle tea
- Collect 1kg of nettle leaves in spring and put them in a bucket with 10 litres of water, ideally rainwater if possible. Weigh down with a brick and leave for 2–4 weeks. The liquid can then be watered down 1 part feed to 10 parts water and fed to your plants.

- You can also make comfrey tea using this method, using 15 litres of water to a kilo of leaves and leaving for 4–6 weeks, but the resulting liquid should be used undiluted.

Tips on feeding

- High-nitrogen feeds will contribute to lush green growth, so are good for leafy greens but not so good for your root veg, which may produce lots of tops and not so much root if overfed nitrogen.

- High-potassium feeds are often referred to as high 'potash'. Tomato feed is an example of a high-potassium feed, as it aids flowering and fruiting. So it's often useful on many other fruiting plants such as aubergines, beans and strawberries, and is best used from when they start to flower.

- Plants can only draw up nutrients when in active growth, so you only use fertilizers from early spring to late summer.

- Plants can only access nutrients when there is moisture present, so make sure to keep them well watered. Without sufficient water, or in too high concentrations, fertilizers can damage plants' roots.

HOW TO MANAGE PESTS

Bug and weed killers are so widely available, lining the aisles of supermarkets, pound shops and garden centres across the country, that it may be the first or only garden product new gardeners come across. They might seem to present a practical solution to a problem, but these are chemicals that are designed to kill things. For me growing food has become a way to nurture and engage with nature, to bring more life, not less, to my garden, to the soil and hopefully to support creatures in the wider environment. I believe the essence of a garden is that it is alive, and gardening is about having a relationship with that living environment – as changeable, challenging and unpredictable as it may be. Ecosystems are a delicate web of connections and interactions. If you put something that is designed to kill things into the system, it's very unlikely to limit its effect to just the one thing you want to remove.

I use only organic methods to remove pests from my garden. I would rather my plants were nibbled than have no creatures in my garden, but equally I can appreciate first-hand the despair of discovering that slugs have hoovered up your baby seedlings. The key to managing pests is to do it in a way that doesn't harm other wildlife in your garden and to be willing to accept a little damage. Here are my top tips for managing pests:

- **Keep on top of pests by regularly spending time in your garden.** It's much easier to spot and rectify any issues before they get out of hand.

- **Create an environment that is attractive to beneficial insects.** I rarely do anything about aphids or blackfly, knowing that in time the wrens and the ladybird larvae will take care of the issue for me. See the Wildlife section (page 229) for more tips on how to do this.

- **Remove pests by hand where possible.** Wash aphids off with water, or pop out with a torch on a rainy evening to collect and remove slugs and snails.

- **Use organic pest management.** When I do intervene it's in a low-impact, simple way, such as using beer traps for slugs (page 52) or netting to keep off caterpillars.

- **Grow plants as plugs, rather than sowing direct.** Plants are at their most vulnerable when they are tiny seedlings, and this is when pest damage is most devastating. If you can, start seeds in modules or trays off the ground, to protect them during this time.

- **Grow extra seedlings to fill any gaps.** If you have extra, you can then easily pop a new plant in the gap, if any get munched.

Here are some of the most common 'pests' I've had a problem with over the years and some simple organic solutions.

Slugs and snails

- **Remove them by hand:** This remains the most effective way I've found to manage slugs and snails in my small garden. There are two good ways to do this:

- In the winter, snails hibernate in big clusters inside old pots and behind bits of wood, so have a look around your garden, turning over bits and bobs, and remove all the snails you can find.
- In the warmer months, the best time to find slugs and snails is to go out on a wet evening with a torch; you will find they are out and about everywhere. Collect them in a container.
- Dispose of them however you see fit. You can release them into the wild, but bear in mind that research shows that snails have a homing instinct up to 20 metres, so throwing them over the fence is not only a good way to fall out with your neighbours but unlikely to be very effective.

- **Barriers:** Slugs and snails can be deterred by putting materials they don't like crossing around your precious plants. Wool pellets work well around individual plants like courgettes, but can be expensive. The tradition of using broken eggshells to protect plants is a popular one but hasn't been shown to be very effective in studies.

- **Remove debris:** Slugs and snails often hide under old leaves in a veg patch, so try to keep the ground clear by removing old and dead leaves from your plants.

- **Organic slug pellets:** Fortunately, traditional slug pellets made with metaldehyde have been banned in the last few years in the UK, as they were found to pose an unacceptable risk to birds and mammals, an example of how pesticides can cause damage far beyond their target. You will see a lot of organic slug pellets for sale in garden centres. The primary ingredient in these is ferric phosphate, which is a naturally occurring substance, but there is some evidence that the combination of ingredients in organic slug pellets can have adverse effects on earthworms, so it's best used sparingly and as a last resort.

- **Nematodes:** Nematodes are tiny worms that you can buy online to target different pests in the garden. They are mixed with water and showered on to the garden, where they will attack their specific host creature. The most commonly used and widely available nematodes are those that target slugs and caterpillars. They are not available for snails.

- **Beer traps:** Beer traps are remarkably effective for slugs in particular. They are essentially cups of beer that you sink into the ground, with a little lid to stop any rain getting in. The slugs are drawn to the beer, so they will climb in and quickly drown (arguably this is not the worst way to go). Be sure to empty out your slug trap regularly, as it can quickly become packed with slugs and in hot weather the result is far from pleasant.

HOW TO MAKE A SLUG BEER TRAP

You can use the cheapest beer you can find for this, or use a nifty solution my mum has come up with, which is to ask a local bar for the dregs from their drip trays, which is completely free.

THE BASICS

You will need:
A container with a lid, such as a large (500ml) yoghurt tub
Scissors
Beer

1. At its simplest you can take a small container, bury it in the garden and fill it with beer. The only downside is if it rains, when your trap will fill up with water.
2. To make a weatherproof beer trap, use a container with a lid such as a yoghurt tub (if you can find a square one with flat sides it will be even easier to cut the flaps).
3. Just below the top of the container, carefully use a sharp knife or scissors to cut a flap in either side, so that when you pull the flap open it folds down and out like a little ramp.
4. Slugs can be drawn from across the garden towards the beer trap, so don't put it right next to your most prized plants. If anything, use it to draw the slugs away. Dig a small hole and bury the container so that the base of the flaps sits on the soil.
5. Fill the trap with beer to just below where you've cut the holes and replace the lid.
6. Beer traps need emptying every few days, especially in hot weather.

Caterpillars and birds

Caterpillars can rapidly wreak havoc in a cabbage patch. Cabbage white butterflies are the culprits and, as the name suggests, they have a taste for cabbages and their relatives, which include kales, broccoli, Brussels sprouts, and also mustards and nasturtiums. The eggs they lay are extremely tiny, yellow and hard to spot, but can be found on the underside of the leaves. If you happen to find any, brush them off. Otherwise they will soon hatch out into tiny caterpillars that increase in size at an exponential rate and quickly shred your plants. Pigeons are particularly keen on pea shoots and brassicas and will happily sit and munch their way through your plants, and many birds will take berries. The best way to keep butterflies and pigeons off your crops is to net them. You can find netting of varying sizes in any garden centre or online, and you can even buy biodegradable ones now. Netting with larger holes will protect from birds, but a finer net will also protect your crops from butterflies. If covering a large area it's best to make a hoop tunnel or cage to put your net over, then you can weigh down the edges with bricks or stones.

Leaf miners

Leaf miners can be a real pain in an edible garden. They are the larvae of small flies that hatch out and burrow into plants, eating them from the inside out.

- Beet leaf miner affects leafy crops like spinach, chard and beetroot.
  - You can spot beet leaf miners by the burrows they leave inside the leaves, with just the papery surfaces remaining. You often also see little grubs wriggling around inside the leaves.
  - After munching their way through your crop the larvae drop to the soil, pupate and hatch out as flies, ready to lay more eggs. Squashing the larvae when you find them inside the leaves can help

disrupt the cycle. Unless infestation is severe, many plants are able to grow through the worst of it.
- You can also net your crops with a fine mesh to prevent the flies laying their eggs, but this is not always failproof.

- Allium leaf miner affects garlic, leeks and onions.
  - Allium leaf miners burrow into the stems, and you may not find them until you cut open your veg. The damage is often manageable in garlic but is less so in leeks, and in both cases the burrows can let other pests and rot into your alliums.
  - There is little you can do about leaf miners, apart from netting your crop with a very fine mesh. This is not failproof, as the flies are very small and can sneak in, but when I netted my garlic I did have the best harvest I've ever had. So it's certainly worth trying.

Aphids and blackfly

From anecdotal observation I would say that plants that suffer the most from aphid infestations are those that are already weak. Healthy plants are more resilient to pests, and a few aphids on a thriving plant will not be its downfall. Aphids are the basis of the food chain for many other insects in the garden. Ladybirds and their larvae, hoverfly larvae, lacewing larvae, wasps, earwigs, beetles and birds all feed on aphids, and their presence in the garden can actually attract these beneficial insects, so do not ever spray them with pesticides. If the infestation gets extreme, I simply rub them off with my hand under a stream of running water.

3

HOW TO GROW VEGETABLES

My first motivation for having a garden was to grow food. It's still one of the things I love most about it, but I have come to appreciate many other things just as much, like the multitude of insects and birds that visit, the different flowers through the seasons, having lunch in the sunshine, lying on a lounger on my tiny gravel patio surrounded by plants and watching ducks fly over every evening from the nearby creek. My garden doesn't look like an allotment, it is not primarily a vegetable patch, it is a garden with food growing in it. In total I would say about a third of my garden is devoted in some way or another to growing edible plants, and that, for me, is an excellent balance. I also believe that food plants add a lot of beauty in the garden, whether it's the vibrant green leaves of a huge kale in the middle of winter, a plant laden with tomatoes or glossy aubergines, the little allium flowers of chives, the deep purple frilly leaves of red mustard or an archway laden with colourful beans. You can introduce food to your garden in whatever way you want – a single pot or planter, a raised bed, a small vegetable patch or a whole little allotment if you have room. There is something very satisfying about sitting in your garden on a summer day eating a meal it has given you, surrounded by the gentle buzz of insects and the scent of flowers.

Creating a veg patch

Having a dedicated area for growing vegetables can be a great way to get lots of food from a small space and to experience the joy of eating something you've grown yourself. Many plants thrive when grown directly in the ground, where there is more consistent moisture, more nutrients and more room for their roots to spread out.

Where to put it

Choose the sunniest spot in your garden for your vegetable patch. Avoid areas that are waterlogged, as most veg plants do not enjoy soggy roots. If you have heavy wet soil everywhere, raised beds are the best solution. Avoid putting your veg bed near to large trees or hedges, as these can easily steal nutrients intended for your plants. A sunny, open site is great, and if you have a fence that doesn't cast shadow on the patch this can be extremely useful for growing plants vertically and creating a little heat trap.

Marking out your beds

Once you've decided where you want to put your veg patch, mark out the size you want your beds to be. Remember to include adequate paths so you are able to get in and tend to plants easily. Use twine and canes to mark out the area, and check that you've made your paths wide enough to walk along easily. Don't make your beds wider than you can reach – if you have access from both sides then make sure you can reach the middle, as this avoids the need to clamber in to tend to your plants.

Paths

At their simplest, you can leave your paths as grass, but bear in mind that the grass will need to be cut and kept in check to stop it spreading into your beds. Another popular option is to lay mulch such as bark or wood chips down on the paths.

How to make brick paths

For my own vegetable beds, I have opted to divide the area up with brick paths, which are both cost-effective and attractive. I've kept it really simple and have made the paths only one brick wide to maximize the space of my beds, keep the cost of materials down and make construction super easy.

You will need:
Bricks (I used clay brick pavers, which are cheaper than building bricks)
Builders' sand
A spirit level
A rubber mallet
A spade

1. First mark out where you want your paths to go and work out how many bricks you'll need.
2. Dig a trench the length you want your path to be, to the depth and width of your bricks, then tread down the trench to compact the soil. Ensure the trench is even across its length, using a spirit level.
3. Evenly fill the base of the trench with a couple of centimetres of builders' sand. Put your first brick in at one end and tap firmly across the surface with the mallet, making the top of the brick level with the soil on either side.
4. Add the next brick and use the mallet to firm it in, lining it up with the first brick. Continue adding bricks and firming them in, using the spirit level to check the height as you go.
5. You may need to add or remove a little builders' sand as you go, to make everything level.

6. When you've completed your path, rub a few handfuls of builders' sand into the joins between bricks to fill the gaps. Brush off any excess with a garden broom.

Preparing the soil

Now that you have your beds marked out it's time to prepare the ground. When establishing a bed for the first time, I prefer the 'no-dig' method popularized by the brilliant gardener Charles Dowding to more traditional methods, which involved digging any added organic matter into the soil with a spade. No-dig keeps things nice and simple by suppressing weeds with cardboard and just adding your organic matter on top. My own veg patch wasn't very weedy after I laid my paths, so I simply skipped the cardboard and topped with fresh compost ready to plant.

How to prepare a no-dig bed

You will need:
Large sheets of cardboard (avoid printed card and remove any tape)
Peat-free compost or mulch
Bark or wood chips for paths (optional)

1. When preparing a new bed on a grassy or overgrown area, remove any stubborn perennial or deep-rooted weeds such as brambles and dandelions. Use a strimmer or lawnmower to cut back the remaining grass and weeds.
2. Cover the area with sheets of cardboard. This will starve the remaining weeds of light. If you haven't built brick paths and simply want to leave mulch paths between your beds, cover the entire area with card, then mark out where you want your beds to go on top.

3. If you plan to start planting straight away, water the cardboard well where you've marked out the beds, to soften it.
4. To create the beds, top the card with about 10–15cm of organic matter such as homemade or shop-bought peat-free compost. For the paths cover with 5–10cm of bark or wood chips.
    Water your beds well and they are ready to plant. You can plant young plants or seeds directly into the top layer of compost. The cardboard will gradually break down and the roots can grow through into the soil below.
5. Key to no-dig is avoiding disturbing the soil – I use a hand hoe to keep weeds down.
6. In the autumn when I clear my summer crops, I top my beds with fresh compost to feed the soil for the next season.

RAISED BEDS

Raised beds are also a popular option in the veg patch, as elevating the planting area improves drainage and makes them easier to access. You can put raised beds directly on soil where they only need to be shallow, as plants can grow down into the ground below, or they can be used on paved areas to create larger beds than allowed by pots, in which case you will want to opt for something deeper. Raised bed kits are widely available, or you can make your own.

Raised beds on a patio

If your area is paved and you want to step up from pots and containers to a larger growing area, raised beds could be a good option. You'll want to get beds 30cm deep or more to give you the option to grow a wide range of vegetables. A metal raised bed kit is probably the most cost-effective option, and many come in packs which can be configured into different shapes depending on what you want in your space. On my own little patio I've gone for a raised bed on legs that is just 40 x 120cm and is a great entry point into growing in larger containers while remaining compact.

How to fill a raised bed

If your raised bed is only shallow and placed on open soil, you can prepare the bed in the same way as you would a regular no-dig bed. Fill the inside base of the raised bed with cardboard to suppress any weeds and top with compost (as detailed above), using a slightly deeper layer of 15–20cm so that your beds are sufficiently full. If you want to put mulched paths around your beds, it is best to cover the area, including paths, with cardboard before putting the raised bed on top, as this will help prevent weeds popping up at the edges of the bed.

If you are putting raised beds on a patio they will need filling from scratch and will require a lot more soil. This can be expensive, but there are ways to reduce the cost, like ordering compost in bulk, or using the hügelkultur method (see below).

FILL A RAISED BED CHEAPLY

Hügelkultur ('mound culture' in German) is an ancient cultivation method that will allow you to fill raised beds cheaply with free organic material you may already have. The base of the bed is layered with logs, then with branches and plant waste (like grass clippings and veg scraps), then topped with compost and garden soil. The idea is that as the wood breaks down it retains water a bit like a sponge, keeping the bed moist, while nutrients are released at different speeds from the varying layers of organic matter.

Even when I'm not doing all the stages of a hügelkultur bed, I find old wood, garden scraps and partially broken-down compost a great way to fill up space in the bottom of large pots and raised beds.

You will need:
Wood (small logs, twigs and branches are ideal, especially older ones which will rot down quicker – but be careful not to disturb existing wildlife; do not use treated manufactured wood)
Green waste (grass clippings, kitchen veg scraps)
Brown waste (cardboard, paper, dry leaves or straw)
Topsoil or multipurpose compost

1. First fill the base of the raised bed about one-third full with wood, branches and twigs. Using the largest pieces at the bottom, pack it all together tightly and water it. As wood breaks down it draws nitrogen out of the soil, which your plants will need to grow. So top the wood with a nitrogen-rich layer of green waste, such as grass clippings, well-rotted manure or veg scraps. There's loads of things you can put in your hügelkultur depending on what you have available, including partially composted material from your compost bin, dry leaves and straw.
2. For your final layer, you want to make sure you have at least 20cm of good-quality potting medium – you can use a combination of old compost, homemade compost, garden topsoil or new shop-bought peat-free compost.
3. Now your bed is ready to plant directly into the top layer.

GROWING FOOD IN POTS

Don't worry if you don't have space for a vegetable garden or if you only have a small patio with no open soil. There are loads of veg you can grow in pots, in fact so many things thrive in pots that I like to grow at least half the food in my garden that way. (Check out my top tips for growing in containers on page 18.) Many of the vegetable projects here are perfect for container growing, including a mangetout tower (page 133), potatoes in containers (page 141), carrots in a bucket (page 137), cucumbers in a window box (page 104), tomatoes in a hanging basket (page 82) and many more, as well as all the fruit projects in this book.

Small pots: These are best for small plants that you only need a little of at a time, such as herbs. You can use several small pots to plant a range of different herbs.

Medium pots: Medium pots are a good home for small, space-saving crops, such as spring onions, a single chilli plant, a selection of two or three different herbs, or strawberry plants.

Large pots and buckets: These are best for plants that need plenty of root room or are especially large, like potatoes, sweet potatoes, tepees of climbing beans, carrots and beetroots. In my opinion it's a waste to grow small shallow-rooted plants like lettuces in a large, deep pot, because you aren't making the most of the precious compost.

Window boxes: These offer a good surface area to volume ratio, by which I mean you can fit in quite a lot of plants without having to use too much potting mix. Window boxes are great for a wide range of plants, such as strawberries, chillies, herbs, trailing tomatoes, spinach and salad leaves. You can even attach a trellis and grow climbing plants like beans, cucumbers and cucamelons.

Grow-bags: The benefit of grow-bags is that they are wide and shallow, making them good for large plants that have shallow roots like tomatoes, courgettes and cucumbers, which can happily spread out. The main issue with taller plants in grow-bags is supporting them – you can buy handy frames to go round your grow-bags which will hold a cane, or use strings if you have something to attach them to.

Hanging baskets: Great for strawberries, trailing tomatoes and nasturtiums – just avoid plants that get too tall. The beauty of a hanging basket is that you can fill it with things that will trail over the sides.

Spacing

Seed packets often come with spacing instructions based on a traditional row system. This isn't very practical in smaller spaces or when planting in containers, so many vegetable gardeners (myself included) will plant at a closer spacing, and in a grid pattern rather than leaving big gaps between rows.

Spacing is also something that can be altered depending on the outcome you want. For example, a packet of spicy salad leaf mix usually includes seeds of things like red mustard, mizuna and pak choi. If sown thickly in a pot or tray these plants will remain small and can be harvested as little salad leaves. But the same seeds can be spaced out and allowed to grow into large individual red mustards or pak choi, and the same is true for lettuces.

Believe it or not, experimenting with spacing can become one of the great creative joys of gardening once you've got a bit of experience. I love the puzzle of combining different plants in different containers and beds at optimal times and spacing to see what's the most I can get out of a small space.

It doesn't always work, but that's the fun of experiments. You start with a theory, you test it out, you learn in the process. Don't let the fear of failure stop you from having the joy and freedom of experimenting.

JUST GET SOWING

My final biggest tip for growing veg, especially during spring and summer, is just remember to get sowing and keep doing it regularly. It's easy to put off sowing veg seeds, but if you have 10 minutes, pop into the garden, fill a tray with compost and chuck in some seeds. In a few weeks' time, when you have plants ready to pop into containers and spaces in your veg patch, you'll be so grateful you did. It's better to do it well enough, than put off doing it completely because you think it has to be perfect.

Veg garden projects

SALAD LEAVES

Lettuce may not seem like the most exciting veg, but not only is it an absolute staple in my garden, it's also brilliantly varied, stunningly beautiful and really good value for money. It falls into that ideal category of veg that is expensive to buy but easy to grow. Bought from the shop, it so often ends up in the bin after half an opened bag goes limp at the back of the fridge. It's the perfect thing to pick fresh as and when you need it, and there are varieties that can be grown all year round. You have two options for growing your lettuce – if you want a harvest quickly and only have limited space, sow thickly in shallow trays to get baby salad leaves. If you want larger, crunchier lettuce leaves then it's better to plant them in a larger container or in the ground; they will take longer to produce but give you bigger harvests.

PROJECT: GROW A VERTICAL SALAD BAR

Using shelves is a great way to save space in a small garden while giving yourself plenty of fresh salad on tap. But this project also works if you want to have a go at sowing a single tray of salad. Many seed companies sell a variety of salad leaf mixes which will include various lettuces, mustards in red and green, rocket, herbs and more. Delicious. Get a few different packets and sow a different one in each tray, to give you the most variety.

When to do it:
Spring and autumn is ideal; it can also be done in the summer, but heat can stress the plants more and dry the trays out quickly. If you want to try this in summer, put the tray in partial shade, out of the heat of the midday sun.

Time from planting to harvest:
4–6 weeks.

You will need:
3 different salad leaf seed mixes
3 seed trays, ideally 30 × 20cm or larger
Peat-free multipurpose compost
Shelving – ideally something that allows light on to each level (optional for making a tower of multiple trays)

How to do it:
1. Make sure your seed trays have drainage holes, then fill them with multipurpose compost to a couple of centimetres below the edge. Sprinkle a couple of pinches of your chosen salad seed

evenly across the surface of the tray. Note: you won't need a whole packet to do a tray, usually ¼ to ½ a packet is enough. Repeat with a different seed mix for each tray.
2. Lightly cover your seeds with another 1cm of compost, then water by either sitting the trays in water, or using a watering can (with a rose attachment to prevent the seeds being washed away).
3. Place your trays of salad on the shelves in a sunny position and keep them moist. Salad leaves will pop up in just a few days in warm weather and can be harvested in as little as 4 weeks.
4. There are two ways to harvest your baby salad. The first is to pick just a few leaves from each plant as and when you need it – the plants will continue growing and will give you a constant supply. The second is to harvest the whole tray in one go, using a pair of scissors to cut the plants a couple of centimetres above the base. After a couple of weeks, the tray will be ready to harvest again.
5. Each tray will usually give you salad greens for about a month, so to have a continuous supply, plant a new tray every couple of weeks.

PROJECT: GROW YOUR OWN CAESAR SALAD

If they take longer and need more space, why bother growing whole lettuce? Because only bigger lettuces have that wonderful refreshing crunch of more substantial leaves, and growing a lettuce with a proper dense heart feels like a real gardening achievement. For whole lettuces I like to start my plants in little plugs or soil cubes. Then I can plant them out in my container or in the ground at the final spacing I want. I always sow extra so I can fill any gaps left after the slugs and snails have had their lunch. I grow lots of different heading lettuces, but to get dense hearts from the smallest space Little Gem is your best bet – and great for a Caesar salad.

When to do it:
Start seeds mid-spring to plant out in late spring (avoid sowing in mid-summer, when it's often too hot for happy lettuce).

Time from planting to harvest:
10–12 weeks.

You will need:
Little Gem seeds
Small module tray or seed tray
Peat-free multipurpose compost
Space in a veg patch or container (a 30cm square is enough space to grow 4 Little Gems)

How to do it:
1. Sow your seeds either individually in small modules or lightly in a small seed tray, ½cm

HOW TO GROW VEGETABLES

deep in multipurpose compost. From mid-spring lettuce can be germinated outside, ideally in a cold frame, mini greenhouse or with a propagator lid on top. This way the plants need no hardening off as they have started life outside. Sow at least twice as many seeds as you need, because extra plants are always useful in the battle against slugs and snails.

2. When your little seedlings have 4–6 leaves it's time to plant them out. Either plant them into the veg patch, or in a container filled with multipurpose compost at a spacing of 15cm between plants. If using modules these can be dropped straight into a small planting hole. To remove seedlings from a seed tray, water well, then gently lift the plants by pushing the handle of a kitchen fork or spoon underneath the seedling and lifting it, holding on to a leaf, not the stem. Gently drop the roots into a small planting hole and firm down.

3. My main protection from slugs and snails is to remove them whenever I see them in the garden, but you could also surround your seedlings with some wool pellets or place a beer trap nearby. Be prepared, especially in spring when your seedlings are small, to replace a few plants. Keep the extra seedlings you've sown and pop them in when any of your original plants fall foul of hungry critters.

4. Keep your plants well watered, especially in dry weather. Your lettuce is ready to harvest when you can feel a firm heart formed inside – this takes around 10–12 weeks. If you notice your plants getting a little cramped together, you

can pull out every alternate plant to help the remaining ones form bulkier hearts.
5. If you aren't intent on growing a dense lettuce head you can start to harvest leaves from your lettuce much sooner, taking the leaves from the outside and leaving the centre to regrow. This way you can pick leaves every week for an extended period. Looseleaf lettuces like Butterhead and Salad Bowl are perfect for this, as they do not form a compact head.

HOW TO EAT THEM:
LITTLE GEM CAESAR SALAD

If I'm going to grow whole lettuces, which take a little longer and are all gone in one picking, I want to make sure they are the star of the show. A home-grown Little Gem Caesar wedge salad is a joy, and it's really easy.

Serves 2 as a side dish

- 1 tinned anchovy fillet
- ¼ of a clove of garlic, crushed
- 1 teaspoon white wine vinegar
- 2 tablespoons mayo
- A handful of grated Parmesan
- Salt and black pepper
- 1 Little Gem lettuce, cut into long wedges
- Croutons (optional)

In a bowl, mash the anchovy fillet to a paste and combine with the garlic and white wine vinegar.

Stir in the mayo and add the Parmesan. Season to taste with salt and pepper. You want a pouring consistency, so add a few drops of water if required.

Drizzle the dressing over your wedges of baby gem and top with a few extra anchovy fillets and croutons if you so desire.

TOMATOES, THE BASICS

If I had just one pot to grow edible plants in, I would choose to grow tomatoes. Despite gardening without a greenhouse for many years and living in the often dreary and unpredictable climate of London, I have harvested tomatoes every year for well over a decade. They are great for beginners, easy to start from seed and even easier to find as young plants in every local garden centre and large supermarket when late spring rolls around. They come in a huge variety of colours, shapes and sizes and have a range of different growth habits. By late summer, with any luck a plant will keep you in continuous tomatoes for several months, and if you have space for several plants you can easily end up with a glut, perfect for turning into sauce or keeping in the freezer to remind you of a little captured summer sun in the middle of winter. While both the projects in this section are in containers, vining tomatoes simply grown up bamboo canes in the veg patch are also a must in my garden every year.

Choosing your tomato

Not all tomatoes grow the same way — some are long and vining and need support (known as indeterminate) and some form sprawling bushes which can be left to spill out of a hanging basket or container with minimal fuss (known as determinate or bush). When deciding which variety of tomato to grow from seed or buy as a plant, here are a few tips:

- If you are growing your tomatoes outside, look for varieties that perform well outdoors. Typically smaller-fruited cherry tomatoes are most likely to ripen outdoors.

- The majority of tomatoes fall into the vining category and will need support, which may seem like a bit of a faff, but vining tomatoes include many of the tastiest varieties and will continue to produce over a longer period than bush varieties.

- If you are growing them in a hanging basket or want a tomato that will spill over the sides of a container, look out for plants that are described as trailing, hanging basket or dwarf varieties.

- Pick something fun! Tomatoes come in loads of colours, shapes and sizes, and trying these out is part of the fun of growing your own.

PROJECT: GROW YOUR OWN TOMATO PLANTS FROM SEED

When to do it:
Early to mid-spring.

Time from sowing to planting out:
Approx. 8 weeks.

What you need:
Tomato seeds
A seed tray, pot or module tray with drainage holes
A propagator, sheet of glass or clear plastic bag
Seed compost or peat-free multipurpose compost

Optional:
Vermiculite
A heated mat or heated propagator
A grow-light

How to do it:
1. Fill your container with seed compost or multipurpose compost with any large pieces removed, up to 1cm below the top of the container.
2. Place your tomato seeds on top of the compost and cover with either a light layer of compost, not more than ½cm deep, or a little sprinkle of vermiculite. Tomato seeds ideally want light to germinate, so it's important not to sow them too deep.
3. Place your tray or pot in a dish of water and let the compost soak up the water until it's damp all the way to the top of the soil.

4. Pop your tray or pot into a propagator with a lid, or inside a large resealable sandwich bag, or cover with a sheet of glass to keep the moisture in.
5. To speed up the germination process you can use a heated propagator or heat mat. This will keep the seeds nice and warm at around 18–21°C and will mean they can germinate in just a few days, as opposed to 1–2 weeks without heat. If using a heat mat it's especially important to cover your seeds, to prevent them drying out.
6. Once your seedlings have appeared, remove any lids or coverings and ensure the seeds are in a light location. This could be a sunny windowsill, or you can use a grow-light to give your plants an extra boost.
7. Don't worry if your seedlings grow long spindly stems, as this can easily be remedied when you pot them up, but do try to rotate the plants daily to stop them leaning too heavily towards the sun in a single direction.
8. Pot your seedlings up into individual 9cm pots when they are about 10cm tall and have at least one set of true leaves. If you've multi-sown your seeds in a tray or pot, simply use the handle of a kitchen fork to ease the plants out from under the roots while gently lifting them by the leaf. If you have sown your seeds individually in modules, you can pop them out and put them into larger pots, burying any long leggy stems below the soil and leaving a couple of centimetres between the top of the soil and the first set of leaves. Tomato plants will happily form new roots on any buried sections of stem.

9. Tomatoes are tender plants, meaning they cannot tolerate frost, so when all risk of frost has passed in your area, make sure to harden them off before you put them outside (see page 32).

PROJECT: GROW A TRAILING TOMATO HANGING BASKET

Growing tomato plants that don't need pruning is a great and easy introduction to this fantastic fruit. An abundance of tomatoes spilling out of a hanging basket is fun and ornamental, as well as a great use of space. The key thing is to get a tomato variety that is suitable for a hanging basket.

When to do it:
Late spring/early summer, after all risk of frost has passed.

Time from planting to harvest:
Approx. 2–3 months to start fruiting.

You will need:
A trailing/hanging basket tomato plant (shop-bought or grown yourself from seed)
A hanging basket (the larger the better, to give your plants room to grow) and a liner such as coir
A hanging basket bracket
Peat-free multipurpose compost

Varieties to try:
Hundreds and Thousands
Tumbling Tom (red or yellow)
Cherry Falls

How to do it:
1. Fix your hanging basket bracket in an open sunny spot on a south-facing wall or at the top of a sturdy fence post.

2. Make sure your hanging basket has drainage holes – some wicker baskets have a plastic liner with no holes, in which case, cut some. If using a coir liner, it's ready to plant.
3. Fill your hanging basket with multipurpose compost. You can add a little slow-release fertilizer such as blood, fish and bone if you have it, but don't worry if you don't.
4. Plant one tomato plant in the centre of your hanging basket and firm it in. Water well.
5. Top your hanging basket with mulch to help retain water – you can use bark chips, gravel or straw.
6. Your tomato will not need any training. Simply keep it well watered, which in very hot weather may mean once or twice a day, and feed it every 1–2 weeks once it starts to flower with an organic high-potassium feed, such as one formulated for tomatoes.
7. Your tomatoes are ready to harvest when they have turned their final colour evenly all over. The tomatoes will ripen at different times, so just pluck them off the plant as and when and enjoy them as soon as possible.

PROJECT: GROW A VINING TOMATO TOWER IN A POT

Growing vining tomatoes can be a little more fiddly, as they require pruning, but the rewards are great. These include some of the tastiest toms and will produce for months. This project works best in a very large pot (50cm across or more) and allows you to create a tall column of tomatoes using several plants in one pot. My preferred tomato for this project is a variety called Sungold, which is prolific and resilient. It also produces extremely sweet tomatoes which often ripen earlier than other varieties. Vining tomatoes are also great in the veg patch, where they can be grown up bamboo canes sunk into the ground.

When to do it:
Spring, after all risk of frost has passed.

Time from planting to harvest:
Approx. 2–3 months to start fruiting.

You will need:
3 vining cherry tomato plants
A large pot, ideally 50cm across
Soil-based or peat-free multipurpose compost
3 × 2.4 metre bamboo canes
Twine
Drainage material

Varieties to try:
Sungold
Gardener's Delight
Black Cherry

How to do it:
1. Cover the base of your pot with drainage material, such as broken pots, gravel or pebbles, then fill up with potting soil. Multipurpose compost is perfectly fine to use, but a soil-based mix will give you greater stability. You can even use a bit of both, depending on what you have.
2. Position the 3 bamboo canes evenly around the edge of the pot and push them down to the bottom of the pot. Cross the canes over, 10cm from the top, and secure with twine.
3. Water your tomato plants well, then remove from their pots and plant one next to each cane, burying it 5cm deeper than the original pot – any buried stem will produce new roots.
4. Secure each plant to the cane with twine. The stems will thicken over time, so don't tie it too tightly – a loose loop is fine. Water in.
5. You can add a layer of mulch, such as bark, gravel or straw, to the top of the pot to aid water retention.
6. Continue to tie the tomato plants to the cane as they grow.
7. In order to make sure these plants don't get too bushy and out of control, it's best to prune them in what's known as a cordon. This involves removing side shoots so that the plants grow as a single main stem. When you see side shoots appearing, simply pinch them out with your fingers. You are looking for the shoot growing in the gap between the main stem and the leaf – the drawing on the following page shows you how to tell which part is a side shoot so you don't get confused and pinch out the wrong bit.

It's best to keep on top of this when the side shoots are small, as they will rapidly grow and in turn start to grow side shoots of their own, which can make it quite confusing. If you have any side shoots that have reached 10cm long or more before you spot them, don't worry, these are perfect for making free tomato plants (see page 89).

8. When the plants reach the top of the canes, pinch out the tops. Keep well watered (if the weather is hot, pots can dry out in a day or two) and feed every 1–2 weeks with an organic liquid feed formulated for tomatoes. Harvest tomatoes as and when they are ready.
9. At the end of the season, in mid- to late autumn, tomatoes will naturally slow down and die either from blight (a common fungal infection that usually arrives at the end of the season) or from cold. It's fine to chop up your plants and add them to the compost heap, as blight doesn't persist long in soil.

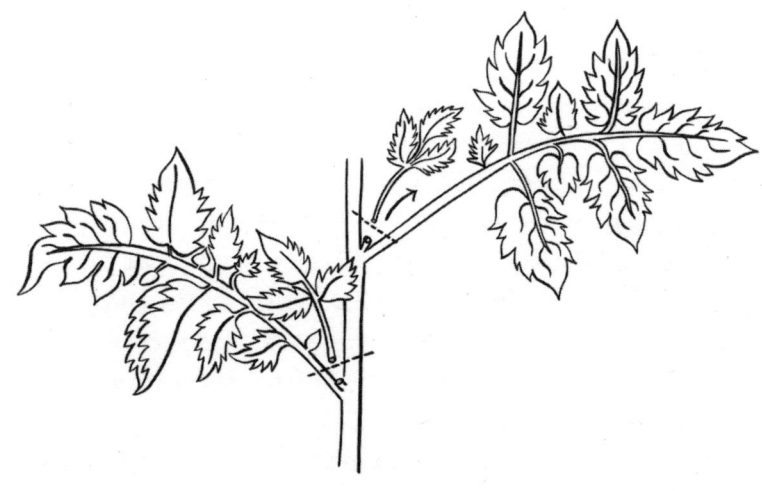

PROJECT: MAKE FREE TOMATO PLANTS

If you've started your tomatoes early in the season, you will have time to make use of the side shoots that you remove from your plants when pruning.

When to do it:
Late spring to early summer, when your plants are large enough to produce side shoots but there is still enough of the season left to make it worth starting new plants. These side shoots will have a good 3–4 week start on new plants started from seed, so can be propagated 4–6 weeks beyond the final tomato sowing date in your area.

You will need:
A tomato plant with side shoots 10cm long or more
A glass of water
9cm pots
Peat-free multipurpose compost

How to do it:
1. Remove the side shoots from your larger plants (see page 87). You can start plants from virtually any size of side shoot, but to get the most mature plants the biggest side shoots will work best.
2. Simply pop them into a glass of water with as much of the stem submerged as possible.
3. After just a few days you will notice bumps appearing on the stem, which will soon burst into new roots, ready to pot up in a week or two.

4. Pot the plants up into individual pots of multipurpose compost and allow them to grow on until the roots fill the pot.
5. If the weather is warm outside and the side shoots are from plants that are already growing in the garden, it's fine to leave them outside in a sheltered spot to grow on before planting out. If your side shoots have come from plants still living indoors, keep them inside and harden them off when all risk of frost has passed.

FRENCH BEANS, THE BASICS

French beans, with their slender round pods, are for me the queen of beans – the most expensive to buy in the shops, the most gourmet in the kitchen and I think the easiest to grow. You can also get them in a range of coloured pods, foliage and flowers, including yellow and purple, which look lovely in the garden. As with most hungry food crops, beans are happiest in a nice sunny spot, with rich well-drained soil that has plenty of added organic matter, but they also grow extremely well in pots.

Choosing your beans

French beans come in two types:

Climbing: As the name suggests, these beans climb, and they can get very tall if grown up an archway, a trellis or just up strings. They produce beans continuously for months and are the best ones to grow in a small space. From a small footprint you get big prolific plants that will give you a regular harvest. Last year I planted just 5 climbing beans in a little patch of ground next to an archway and had beans on tap every few days for several months.

Dwarf: Unlike climbing beans, dwarf French beans are bushes that get to around 45–60cm tall and produce the majority of their beans in the first flush, which happens roughly in one go, so you get a nice big harvest. With a bit of care and a good feed they will continue to produce more beans, but they won't produce for as long as climbing beans. Dwarf beans grow quickly, either in the ground or in a pot, and are my favourite way to fill gaps in the garden in mid- to late summer. In the UK they can be sown direct through to late summer, to give you a harvest before the first frost.

PROJECT: FILL YOUR FENCE WITH CLIMBING BEANS

This method works best on fences that have the backer rails on your side of the garden, as these provide a sturdy point for securing the top of your support. If you are using bean plants, give them a good water before planting them out. If you don't have a fence, climbing French beans can also be grown up a bamboo tepee (see page 25), either in a large pot or at the back of the veg patch to prevent overshadowing lower-lying veg, or you can make them into a feature on an archway in a sunny spot in the garden.

When to do it:
Early summer when all risk of frost has passed.

Time from planting to harvest:
10–12 weeks.

You will need:
Climbing French bean plants or seeds
Strong string
Nails approx. 5–6cm long
A hammer
A sturdy fence in a sunny spot
Organic matter such as multipurpose compost

Varieties to try:
Carminat (purple)
Cobra (green)
Monte Gusto (yellow)

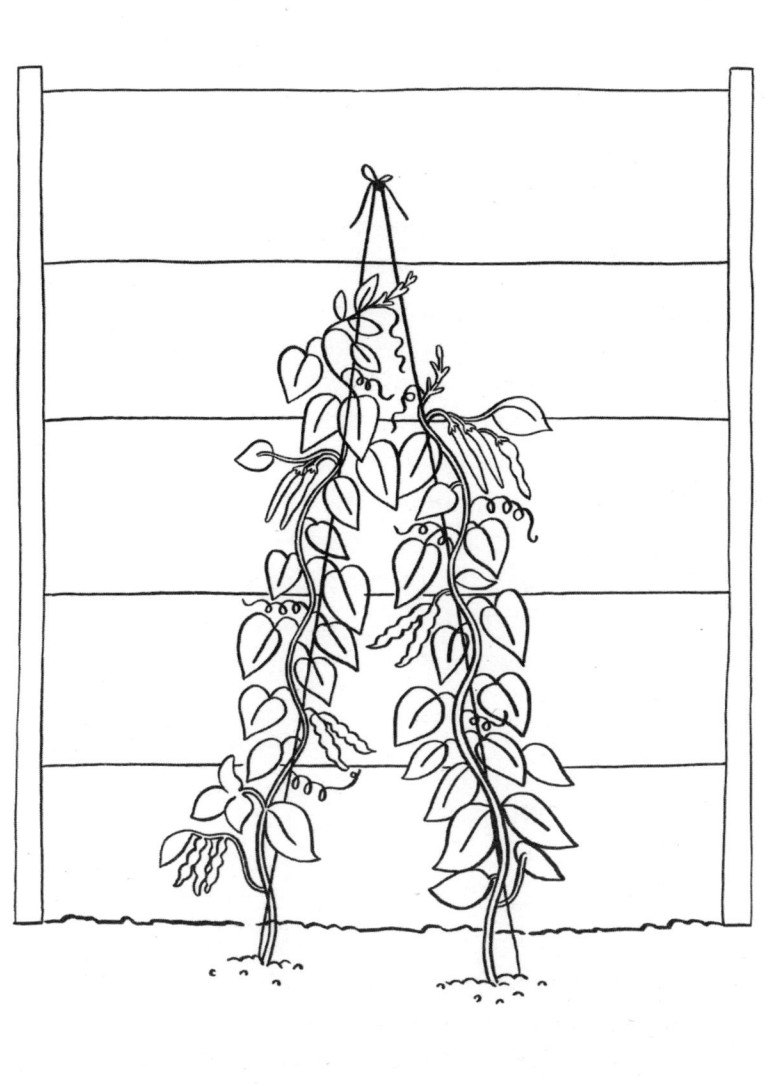

How to do it:
1. Find a sunny spot in front of your fence in your prepared veg bed, or, if using a new patch of ground, clear any weeds. You want to position your beans 15cm apart. Work out how many plants you can fit into the space and then allocate one nail to each 2 plants.
2. Hammer your nails halfway into the top backer rail on your fence, spacing them 30cm apart and making sure they are secure.
3. If you do not have a backer rail on your side of the fence, you have a couple of options. If there is a backer rail on the other side, hammer your nails into the slats, with the backer rail behind so you don't leave exposed nails poking out on your neighbour's side of the fence. If there are no backer rails, pop a screw at the top of each of your fence posts and attach a strong wire between them. You can tie your strings at intervals along the wire, instead of tying them to nails.
4. Take a long piece of string a little more than twice the length of the height of your fence. Find the middle of the string and tie it around the nail, so that you have two long strings either side, which reach the ground with a little excess at either end.
5. Dig two holes in the ground, one either side of the position of the nail above. Then pop one end of the string into the bottom of the hole, and the other end into the other hole.
6. Add a few handfuls of multipurpose compost, homemade compost or well-rotted manure to each planting hole and gently dig it in. If planting

7. Plant one bean seed or plant in the soil, on top of the string. Seeds should be sown 4cm deep. Firm in and water well. If using plants, loop the top of the plant gently around the string to help it start climbing.
8. Once planted, your beans won't need a lot of care. The major problem will be slugs and snails, so keep the ground around the base of your plants clear of weeds and leaves where slugs and snails can hide. Consider using wool pellets around the base of your plants. Planting seedlings rather than sowing seeds may also give them a better chance of success against pests.
9. Keep your beans well watered and when they start to flower, feed them every 1–2 weeks with an organic liquid feed high in potassium (those formulated for tomatoes are a good choice).
10. Pick beans regularly to keep them producing more – they are most tender when small and slender (about 10cm long) but can get to 15–20cm depending on variety. If you start to see the shape of the beans through the pod they've gone too far, so pick them immediately – they can still be used but may need more cooking.
11. When the beans reach the top of the support, pinch out the tops to encourage more growth and new flowers lower on the plant.
12. Climbing beans can produce well into autumn, but when it turns cold the plants will naturally die.

PROJECT: SUCCESSION-PLANT WITH DWARF FRENCH BEANS

When it gets to mid- to late summer there is lots to harvest in the garden, but the planting window for many crops has passed. Thankfully dwarf French beans offer a perfect gap filler, providing a harvest of lush tender beans in just 2–3 months. It's one of the most productive things you can do with a spare spot in the veg bed, following a harvest of anything that leaves an empty spot behind, such as early potatoes, lettuce, carrots, beetroot or garlic. The beans can also be grown in pots – I would space 4 plants to a 30cm pot.

When to do it:
Late spring to late summer.

Time from planting to first harvest:
8–10 weeks.

You will need:
Dwarf French bean seeds
Module tray or deep seed tray
Peat-free multipurpose compost
An empty spot in your veg bed

Varieties to try:
Purple Queen (purple)
Ferrari (green)
Boston (green)
Adoration (yellow)

How to do it:

1. If you are feeling super-efficient, you can start your seedlings in trays 2–3 weeks before it's time to harvest your previous crop. So as soon as you harvest the first crop you have plants waiting to fill the gap.
2. Simply fill a module tray or a deep seed tray with multipurpose compost (an old supermarket produce tray with some drainage holes added will work fine!). Sow one seed per module or 10 seeds in a 15 × 10cm produce tray, push your beans in 2–3cm below the surface, cover with compost and water your tray well. As it's summertime your beans will happily germinate outside, but keep them off the ground to help prevent slug damage and don't let them dry out.
3. Once you've harvested your previous crop, it's time to plant out your beans. Water well, and if multi-sown in a tray, gently tease apart the individual plants.
4. Plant them 15cm apart in a row or block, depending on how much space you have, at the same depth they were previously. Water in well.
5. You can also sow beans direct in the ground straight after removing the previous crop. They can be sown direct from late spring to mid/late summer. Simply sow the beans 3–4cm deep, 15cm apart, and water them in. In the warm soil they will pop up in no time.
6. The first flush of beans on dwarf beans is always the best and the largest, but if you feed the plants when they start flowering and pick them regularly you can prolong the harvest period to

several weeks. Beans are ready to pick when they are 10–15cm long and as thick as a pencil.

7. Sow a succession of beans in gaps around the veg patch, or in pots as and when you have a spare space, so that you have a continuous supply.

CUCUMBERS, THE BASICS

Cucumbers can be a little tricky to master. I don't say this to put you off, because when they work they are one of the best crops there is – nothing tastes like a home-grown, freshly picked cucumber, and the plants can be prolific when they are happy. But take some reassurance from the fact that I've killed more cucumbers than any other plant; it's easily done, but no reason to give up on them. They are very sensitive to cold, don't like wet feet and don't bounce back well from being rootbound.

Garden centres often start selling cucumber plants very early in the season, when they might be happy in a heated greenhouse but certainly won't survive outdoors. That was my first experience trying to grow cucumbers. I bought two little plants in very early spring and promptly potted them up into some grow-bags in my parents' garden. My mum, on noticing what I was up to, told me it was far too early for tender things like cucumbers and that they wouldn't survive. I optimistically ploughed on, only to have both plants collapse irreparably a few days later.

So, top tips: take care introducing them to the outside world (see hardening off, page 32), don't put them outside until the weather is warm both in the day and at night, and don't give up on them if you occasionally kill one. Also, listen to your mum. The same year that I killed my first two plants, I went on to grow an absolutely stunning cucumber in a grow-bag up a cane and it had fabulous full-sized cucumbers trailing all down its stem – it was magical.

Choosing your cucumber

Cucumber varieties are specified as suitable either for indoors (greenhouse) or outdoors. As the name suggests, indoor varieties need warmth to fruit successfully and are best grown in a greenhouse or polytunnel. Outdoor varieties, also known as ridge cucumbers, are better suited to outdoor growing and for those with limited space and equipment, which is why I recommend them to anyone trying cucumbers for the first time. If you want to grow them in the veg patch they can be planted out and left to trail to their hearts' content.

Cucumbers come in many more varieties than you are used to seeing at the supermarket. Green, white, round, yellow – there's plenty to have a go at growing. I've always been drawn to the smaller fruits, about half the size of a standard supermarket cuke, or the even smaller miniature or gherkin types that are a perfect snack or garnish for a summer Pimm's or G&T.

Outdoor varieties to try:

Marketmore: Half-sized, thick-skinned and slightly spiny cucumbers with dense, succulent flesh.

Crystal Apple: Very popular with home gardeners, these prolific plants produce crunchy pale green cucumbers that resemble the shape and size of an apple.

Miniature White: A little white gherkin-type cucumber whose plants are very compact, making them good for containers. The fruits are extremely crisp and mildly sweet.

PROJECT: GROWING YOUR OWN CUCUMBER PLANTS FROM SEED

When to do it:
Mid- to late spring – cucumbers grow quickly and don't like the cold, so there is no need to start them too early.

Time from sowing to planting out:
3–4 weeks, plus hardening-off time.

What you need:
Cucumber seeds
Small pots or a module tray
Seed compost or peat-free multipurpose compost, with large pieces removed
Propagator or large clear resealable bag

Optional:
Perlite
Heated propagator

How to do it:
1. Cucumbers need to be started in the warm. A sunny windowsill is ideal, but the boost of a heated propagator will get them going even quicker.
2. Cucumbers don't like to be soggy – adding a little perlite to your peat-free compost can help them stay moist but not too damp.
3. Sow seeds in individual pots or in a module tray with large deep modules, planting the seeds 1cm deep on their long side, rather than flat, as this helps to prevent rotting.

4. Place inside a propagator or pop the pot into a reusable sandwich bag to prevent moisture loss.
5. Seedlings should appear in a week, at which point you need to make sure they get plenty of light on a bright windowsill to prevent them going leggy. But avoid leaving them to bake in full direct sun, especially if the weather is hot.
6. Cucumbers hate the cold, so don't be tempted to move them outside until the weather warms up and all risk of frost has passed, in late spring or early summer.
7. Gradually harden off plants before putting them outside (see page 32).

PROJECT: CUCUMBERS IN A WINDOW BOX

One of my favourite methods for growing my outdoor cucumbers is in a large window box on my patio, with a simple makeshift trellis against the wall.

When to do it:
Early summer, when all risk of frost has passed.

Time from planting to harvest:
6–8 weeks.

You will need:
2 outdoor cucumber plants
A large window box 70cm or more long
3 bamboo canes 1.2 metres or more tall
2 bamboo canes the same length as the longest side of the window box
Drainage material
A piece of plastic mesh trellis, chicken wire or netting the same width as the longest side of the window box and 1 metre or more tall
Twine
Peat-free multipurpose compost

How to do it:
1. Fill the bottom of the window box with drainage material such as broken pots, brick or gravel, then top with compost. Take 2 of the longer bamboo canes and push them into the soil in each back corner of the container.
2. Using the holes in the mesh, feed the edges of the trellis or chicken wire over the bamboo

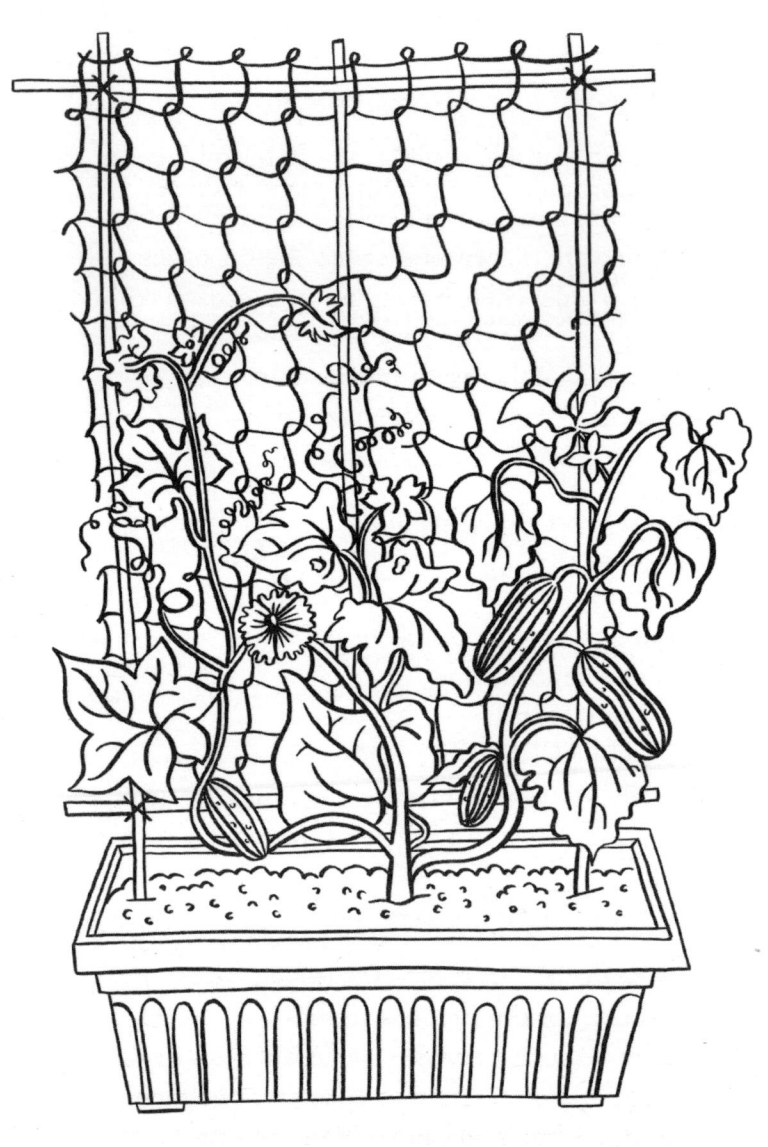

canes, alternating the bamboo canes back and forth through each hole until the trellis is at the bottom of the canes and at the level of the soil.
3. Using the same method, push the shorter bamboo canes horizontally along the top and bottom sides of the trellis. You should now have a window box with a trellis at the back, held in place by a framework of bamboo canes. Tie the canes with some twine where they cross over at each corner. Trim the canes with secateurs if needed.
4. Take the final longer bamboo cane and push it down the middle of the trellis with the bottom of the cane on the outside of the back of the window box.
5. This construction is a simple makeshift job, but when pushed against a wall it will work fine for a season.
6. Plant the 2 cucumber plants 40cm apart. If your window box is too small for this spacing, plant one cucumber instead. Plant them no deeper than they were in their original pots.
7. Cucumbers like consistently moist but not waterlogged soil, so water little and often.
8. When they start to flower, feed them with a high-potassium feed, such as one formulated for tomatoes, every 1–2 weeks throughout the growing season.
9. Cucumbers have male and female flowers (similar to courgettes) – only female flowers produce fruit and can be identified by the miniature cucumber behind the flower. If your cucumbers start to flower when the plants are still small, with only a few leaves, it's worth

removing the first few male and female flowers to put more energy into establishing the plant.
10. Tie your cucumbers to the trellis as they grow, and pinch out the tops when they reach the top of the trellis, which will promote side shoots.
11. The size you want to harvest your cucumbers at depends on the variety you planted, so be sure to keep a note of this. The classic outdoor variety I grow every year on a trellis is Marketmore, which is ready to harvest at around 15cm long.
12. Cucumber fruits grow quickly, so keep an eye on them – from the point of flowering they can be ready to pick in a week and a half. If they start to go soft or change colour they have been left too long. Don't be afraid to pick them, it's better to pick them small than leave them too long.

PROJECT: GROW COURGETTES FROM SEED

Courgettes are an absolute must every summer in my garden. They are prolific, and I pick mine from early summer to mid-autumn, adding them to meals every week. The seeds are big and germinate quickly, resulting in huge leafy plants that are soon adorned with big bright yellow flowers that last just a single day, opening in the morning and filling with pollen-dusted sleepy bees, and closing up before the day is out.

The fruits come in many more exciting varieties than the standard green ones you find in the supermarket – they can be bright yellow, pale bulbous green, round ... My personal favourite is a hugely productive half-yellow half-green one called Zephyr, which has an especially delicious sweet flavour when pan-fried in slices with a little olive oil and salt.

One plant is enough for most people's needs, but I always grow several because I can't ever decide on just one variety. Plus more plants mean better pollination, and harvesting a big pile of gorgeous courgettes is never a chore!

When to do it:
Mid-spring to early summer.

Time from sowing to planting:
Approx. 3 weeks, plus hardening-off time.

You will need:
Courgette seeds
9cm pots
Seed compost or peat-free multipurpose compost
A propagator tray with lid, sandwich bag or sheet of glass

Varieties to try:
Atena Polka: A prolific bright yellow courgette.
Zephyr: A must for me every year, pale yellow with a green tip.
Ronde de Nice/Tondo di Nizza: Round green courgettes, perfect for picking small and stuffing.
Bianca di Trieste: Pale green bulbous courgettes.
Defender: Classic dark green courgettes.

How to do it:
1. Fill 9cm pots with seed compost or multipurpose compost, then place one seed on its longest side in each one, 1–2cm deep, and water well, allowing excess water to drain off.
2. Pop into a propagator or into reusable sandwich bags to make sure they don't dry out. Put them in a warm spot on a sunny windowsill, or in a heated propagator if you have one.
3. Courgette seedlings appear in about a week, faster when it's warmer or if germinated on a heat mat.
4. Uncover your seedlings and keep them watered and in a light spot on a sunny windowsill, or under a grow-light. They will rapidly become leggy without enough light, and then there is a risk their delicate stems could snap.
5. Harden them off gradually when all risk of frost has passed (for me that's late spring). Don't be tempted to put them outside too early – tender plants will get a shock from cold miserable weather even if it's not actually freezing.
6. When the weather warms up in late spring you can also germinate your seeds outside, where they will benefit from much higher light levels.

PROJECT: GROW COURGETTES IN A VEG BED

When to do it:
Early summer.

Time from planting to harvest:
Approx. 6 weeks.

You will need:
1 courgette plant of your chosen variety
A 60cm square space in your veg patch
A prepared veg bed (page 58) or some multipurpose compost with a little organic plant food

How to do it:
1. Choose a sunny spot with 60cm square space. Bear in mind that the plants get big, so don't be tempted to plant them too close together, even if they look small now.
2. Dig a small hole in the centre of your patch, twice the size of the pot you've grown your plant in.
3. If you've already prepared your veg bed with plenty of organic matter, the ground is ready to plant. If not, add some multipurpose compost or well-rotted manure and a little blood, fish and bone to the hole, following the packet instructions.
4. Give your courgette a good water, then remove it from its pot and pop it into the hole, ensuring that it's planted at the same depth it was in the pot.
5. Firm the soil gently back around the rootball and water well.
6. If you have one, stick a short bamboo cane into the ground next to the plant, to make it easier to

find the base of the stem for watering later in the summer.

7. Courgettes are hungry plants and it's best to water them with a liquid feed that's high in potassium every week or two once they start to flower (one formulated for tomatoes is ideal). If you notice that the production of flowers and fruits has dropped or stopped, it's a sure sign they need a feed.
8. Courgette leaves are prone to powdery mildew, white patches that appear mostly on the oldest leaves. The best way to keep your plants well aerated and happy is to remove these older leaves from the main stem between where it emerges from the soil and where the fruits are forming.
9. Courgette flowers come in two types, male and female. The female flowers have a baby courgette behind them and the male flowers just a long thin stem. Early in the season it is not uncommon for baby courgettes to shrivel and fall off the plant because they haven't been pollinated. The problem is often caused by male and female flowers not being on the plant at the same time when the plants are still small. You can hand-pollinate by taking an open male flower and dusting the pollen inside the female flower, but if you don't have the male flowers, don't worry – as the plants get bigger and produce more flowers you'll start to get fruit.
10. The first few courgettes tend not to grow as large as later ones, so pick them when they are still quite small (10–12cm long) to promote the plant to produce more. These pickings are a special early treat.

11. Courgettes can grow very quickly, and if you leave them for just a few days you may find a marrow! They are best harvested small and in their prime – about 15–20cm is perfect. Any larger and they can become more watery and less flavoursome, but can still be used in soups and can even be grated to use in cakes.
12. Courgettes continue to produce well into autumn, and usually put on a late burst of fruit at the end of the season when the weather cools down and gets wetter, so don't pull them out too early. Once it gets cold the plants will naturally die.

HOW TO EAT THEM:

Come mid-summer every gardener is desperate for ideas for more ways to cook courgettes. In the middle of winter I can hardly imagine there could be such a thing as too much food from the garden, but every year it happens – the inevitable courgette glut.

Here are a couple of my favourite ways to eat them.

COURGETTE FRITTI

Deep-frying is a faff, but the results are oh, so good. I deep-fry a handful of times a year and I usually reserve this privilege for home-grown produce – sweet potato bhajis, deep-fried courgette flowers and this most summery of treats. One large courgette or 2 medium makes a plateful, and paired with a cold drink in the garden on a summery evening at the end of the working week, it is just pure joy.

Serves 4

> 2 medium courgettes
> 100ml milk
> 100g plain flour, for coating
> Salt and black pepper
> Sunflower oil, for frying
> A good grating of Parmesan

Cut the courgettes into long slices ½cm thick, then cut each slice into strips. Pour the milk into a shallow dish. Put the flour on to a plate and season it with salt and pepper, ready to coat your courgettes.

Now start heating your oil – it's best to use a deep fat fryer if you have one, in which case set it to 180°C. If not, pour 3–4cm of oil into a medium-sized pan, making sure that it isn't more than one-third of the depth of the pan. Preferably use a cooking thermometer to check the oil does not get hotter than 190°C.

Coat the courgettes first in the milk, then in the seasoned flour. Knock off any excess flour. Test the temperature of the oil by dropping in one sliver of courgette – it should bubble and rise to the top of the oil immediately. If it sits on the bottom of the pan the oil is not hot enough, so wait a few more minutes before adding the rest of your courgettes.

Cook the courgettes in a couple of batches, as adding too many at once will cool the oil too quickly and they will take a lot longer to cook. They cook very quickly, taking just a minute or two to go pale golden with a few browner flecks. Scoop them out with a slotted spoon, pop them on to a plate topped with kitchen paper to drain any excess oil, and season with salt immediately.

Pile up your courgetti fritti while still piping hot and grate a generous amount of Parmesan over the top. Serve immediately.

BARBECUED COURGETTES WITH CHILLI, MINT AND FETA

This is a good way to use up lots of courgettes if you find yourself inundated. Nothing is more summery than home-grown courgettes sizzling on the barbecue, with sunlight shining through the barbecue haze.

Serves 6 as a side dish

> 5 medium courgettes, cut in half lengthways (big courgettes can be cut into 3 or 4 thick slices)
> Salt
> ½ a packet of feta, crumbled

Dressing

> 2 teaspoons maple syrup
> 5 large leaves of fresh mint, finely shredded

A pinch of chilli flakes
3 tablespoons extra virgin olive oil
1 tablespoon white wine vinegar
A big squeeze of lemon

Sprinkle the courgettes with salt and leave for 15 minutes.

Combine the ingredients for the dressing in a large bowl, then crumble in the feta and stir to combine. Leave to infuse while you cook the courgettes.

Wipe off any liquid from the courgettes and put them on a super-hot barbecue. Let them blister and char on both sides, turning them repeatedly. You want them to soften a little but still have some bite – when they reach this stage, put the hot courgettes straight into the bowl of feta and dressing and combine until well covered.

This salad is also delicious cold, in which case allow the courgettes to cool before combining them with the dressing.

Serve on a big platter in the middle of the table.

PROJECT: USE A COLD FRAME TO GROW SPINACH AND RADISHES

Cold frames are essentially mini greenhouse boxes with lids, and are extremely useful in the veg patch. They are a cost-effective way to extend your veg season without having to invest in a greenhouse. In early spring they allow you to start crops earlier, and in the summer you can use them to grow low-lying heat-loving plants like melons and sweet potatoes. In the autumn they can be filled with winter salad, which will grow through the cold months with the benefit of a bit of protection.

During the day, cold frames are often much warmer inside than the outside air, and they also protect young seedlings from cold, drying winds. This means that plants grown in a cold frame will have much larger, softer, lusher leaves, compared to those left to grow out in the open. Every spring I sow the same two crops in my cold frame, spinach and radishes. It's a little ritual to mark the beginning of a new year in the garden and gives me a super early harvest of the freshest, lushest crops. Radishes and spinach can germinate in fairly cold conditions, meaning they can be grown direct with a bit of protection as early as late winter/early spring. You can also grow early spring lettuces in the same way.

When to do it:
Mid-spring.

Time from planting to harvest:
6–8 weeks (quicker as the weather warms up).

You will need:

Spinach seeds, such as Cello, Medania, Amazon
Summer radish seeds, such as French Breakfast,
   Diana, Scarlet Globe, or a rainbow mixed packet
A movable cold frame, ideally around 60 × 90cm
Peat-free multipurpose compost
A space in your veg patch big enough for your
   cold frame

How to do it:

1. If you are planting into a prepared veg bed that has recently been topped with organic matter, you don't need to do anything to prepare the ground. However, when sowing direct I find it helps to have a fine, fresh layer of topsoil or compost, so once I've placed my cold frame where I want to grow things I add 3–5cm of peat-free multipurpose compost to create a nice bed for my seeds. This also helps keep down small weed seeds and makes any slugs or snails easier to spot.
2. Be sure to pick a spot that gets plenty of light – the strength of the light is lower in the early spring and your little plants need all the light they can get.
3. Water well before sowing, then divide your cold frame into two sections, half for your spinach and half for your radishes. Make a grid of holes about 1cm deep, 7cm apart for your radishes, then drop 2 seeds into each hole and cover. Do the same for the spinach but space the holes 10cm apart, also sowing 2 seeds per hole.
4. Keep your cold frame lid closed to keep the warmth in. Your seedlings should appear within

a few weeks. If both radish seedlings germinate, thin to a single seedling. Seedlings at this time of year are prime prey for slugs and snails, so you will need to keep a close eye out for them and think about sowing extra seeds in a tray to fill any gaps if they do get eaten.

5. Your seedlings may be slow to get going in the cold weather, but they soon accelerate as light levels and warmth increase.
6. Harvest your radishes when they are 2–3cm across, and remember that the leaves are also edible! They can be a little hairy, but are great cooked up like spinach.
7. Once your spinach reaches 8–10 leaves, it's a good time to thin down to a single plant if both seeds germinated. You can eat these thinnings. Then you can start harvesting the tender leaves from the remaining plants from the outside, leaving just a few of the smallest leaves in the centre, and in a week your plants will be ready to pick again.
8. Spinach and radishes don't like extreme heat, so leave your cold frame lid open on warm days or remove it completely in early summer. As the weather warms up, spinach will go to seed, but you can make the plants last a little longer by removing and using any tall middle stems that appear.
9. By early to mid-summer, harvest any remaining plants and replace with a summer crop. If you want to make use of the cold frame, try sweet potatoes or melons. Or remove the frame and plant courgettes, tomatoes or cucumbers.

HOW TO EAT THEM:

I love quick pickles, and you can use this recipe for all sorts of veg. The intention here is not to preserve, just to create deliciously vinegary flavoursome pickles, so these should be kept in the fridge after you make them. I like my pickles sweet and sour, but you can adjust the amount of salt and sugar as well as the flavourings to your own personal taste. They will keep in the fridge for 1–2 weeks, but I eat them long before that.

PICKLED RADISHES

Makes one 350ml jar

> 15 radishes, approx. 250g (or other garden veg such as cucumbers, carrots, etc.)
> 135ml white wine vinegar
> 135ml water
> 2 teaspoons salt
> 2 tablespoons caster sugar

Flavourings:
> 1 x 2cm piece of ginger, peeled and cut into thin matchsticks
> 1 teaspoon coriander seeds
> A pinch of chilli flakes

Wash the radishes, then remove the tops and bottoms and cut into thin coin-like discs. Put them into the jar, pushing them down to pack in as many as possible.

Put the vinegar, water, salt and sugar into a small saucepan and warm until dissolved, then take off the heat. Add the ginger, coriander seeds and chilli flakes, or other flavourings of your choice.

Allow to cool a little, then pour over the radishes, including the flavourings, until the jar is full and put the lid on.

Once cool, pop the jar into the fridge. The pickles can be eaten after a few hours and I like them crunchy and fridge-cold. If left for a couple of days the colour from the radish skins will dye the slices a beautiful pink.

PROJECT: GROW A CONSTANT SUPPLY OF SPRING ONIONS IN A POT

Spring onions are not expensive to buy, but like herbs and salad they are one of those things that is great to have in the garden as and when you need it, rather than going sad at the bottom of the fridge. There are an array of different colours to try, including purple and red, as well as ones that are hardy for sowing in autumn for spring harvests. This method uses a very small space to grow a constant supply, sown thickly and harvested gradually across a long period of time.

When to do it:
Mid-spring through to mid-autumn.

Time from planting to harvest:
8–10 weeks, but can vary depending on the time of year.

You will need:
A packet of spring onion seeds (or why not try mixing a couple of different colour packets together?)
A 30cm pot
Peat-free multipurpose compost
Drainage material
A pot saucer

Varieties to try:
White Lisbon: Great all-rounder, quick-growing and perfect for autumn sowing.
Lilia: Beautiful purple spring onion.
North Holland Blood Red: Deep red stems.

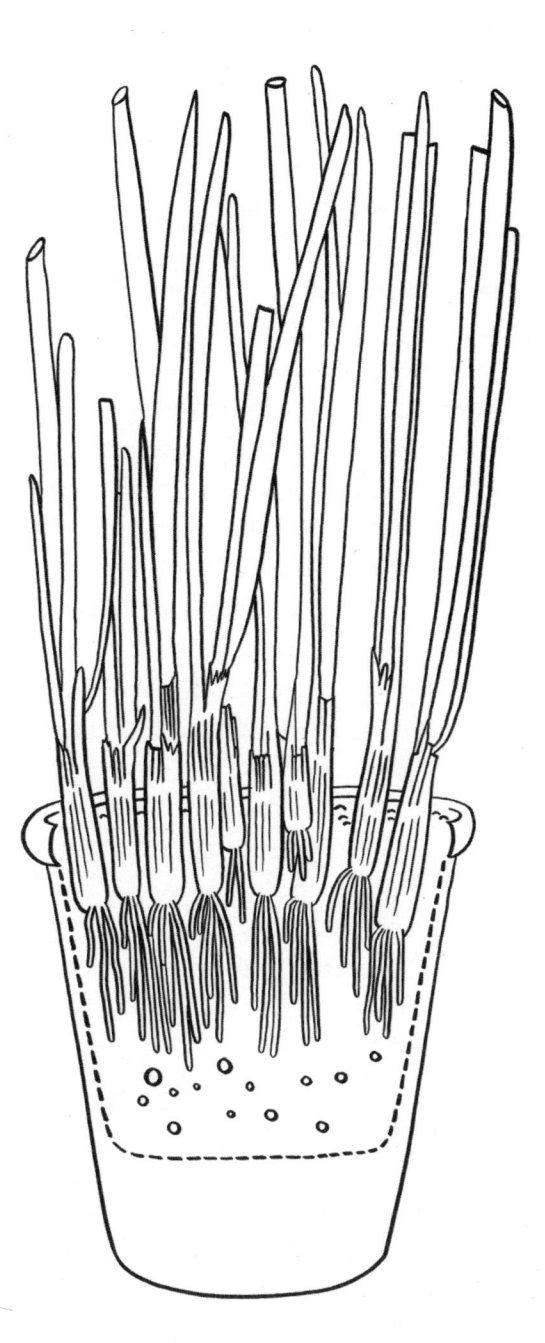

How to do it:
1. Spring onions can be sown early in the year when it's still cool, but they can take a long time to germinate. Sowing when the weather warms up a little will ensure better and faster germination.
2. Fill the base of your pot with some drainage material such as broken pots or gravel, then add your compost up to a couple of centimetres below the edge of the pot.
3. Sprinkle your seeds thickly over the surface of the soil. Don't worry about the spacing instructions on the packet!
4. Cover with 1cm more compost. Water the surface of your pot gently, using a rose attachment to avoid washing your seeds around and leaving them all in one spot.
5. Spring onions germinate best when they are kept moist, but not waterlogged, until they come up. If you have a sheet of glass or a propagator lid you can pop this over the pot to help prevent it drying out. If sowing in the hotter months, without a cover, keep the surface of your soil well watered, especially when the seedlings start to appear. Dry compost can form a crust over the seedlings which can be hard for them to break through.
6. Spring onions can be sown for many months of the year, but those sown at the end of the summer or autumn will grow much more slowly and won't be ready to harvest until the following spring.
7. Your spring onions should grow thickly, looking a bit like a pot of grass initially. When they get ½cm thick, start to pull the baby spring onions,

which you can use as you would chives, making sure to take them evenly from across the pot to make room for the rest to grow.
8. Harvest as and when you need them, taking just a few at a time, and keep them well watered.
9. You can start a second pot a month or two after the first, to have a constant supply.

PROJECT: GROW YEAR-ROUND LEAFY GREENS

Of all the things I grow in my garden, greens are the one I actually pick and use the most. I like to grow a combination of kale, chard and perpetual spinach, all of which can be added to lots of recipes and are super-nutritious.

These greens can all be started in spring, just as the previous year's plants are coming to an end, which means that apart from a small gap while the new plants are establishing, I have them available to pick outside my door all year round. These are all fairly cold-tolerant crops and they are best started outside with protection, where they will benefit from lots of natural light and be already acclimatized to outdoor growing conditions when it's time to plant them in their final location. The great thing is that these seeds can all be started in the same way at the same time, making it an easy job to tick off. Or you can even buy some small plants from the garden centre and bung them straight in, for instant filler. A 60 × 90cm patch in the veg garden is perfect for growing greens all year round, but you can also pop plants into containers or grow them in rows.

When to do it:
Mid-spring to mid-summer (early sowings will benefit from the protection of a propagator lid or greenhouse).

Time from planting to harvest:
Plants are large enough to start harvesting after 2–3 months.

You will need:
Kale seeds
Chard seeds
Perpetual spinach seeds
A seed tray or module tray
Seed compost or peat-free multipurpose compost
A propagator lid (for early sowings)
A 60 x 90cm patch of your vegetable garden

Varieties to try:
KALE:
Curly kale: Perhaps the easiest to grow is curly kale, which seems to be left alone by the majority of pests that plague brassicas. It comes in deep purple as well as green.
Cavolo nero: A beautiful plant, with long narrow wrinkled leaves that are so deep a green they are almost black.
Red Russian kale: This stunning kale has purple stems and soft, serrated green leaves. Super tender and ornamental.

CHARD:
Bright Lights Mixed: The go-to mix, as it contains a variety of different beautiful colours.
Fordhook Giant: Can grow to a very large size, with thick white tender stems.
Rhubarb Chard: Beautiful red stems and vibrant green leaves.

PERPETUAL SPINACH:
Perpetual spinach doesn't come in a range of varieties but may also be called spinach beet or leaf beet.

How to do it:
1. Kale are the largest plants, then chard and finally perpetual spinach. For this project you want to end up with 2 kale plants, 4 chard plants and 6 perpetual spinach plants. But you can adjust the numbers to the space you have.
2. Fill your module or seed tray with multipurpose compost (with large pieces removed) or seed compost. Sow twice as many seeds as you need plants, to make sure you will have enough. Sow all your seeds 1cm deep, either in individual modules or in rows in a seed tray, leaving 2cm between seeds so the little plants have room to grow to a decent size before being transplanted. Make sure to label them, so you know what's what! Water well, then give them some protection if sown early in the year. At its simplest, I start these in seed trays on some shelves in my garden with propagator lids on top. It can get pretty windy in spring, so I pop a little weight on to keep the lids from flying away.
3. From late spring onwards seedlings can be planted out into a prepared veg bed (page 58) when they have at least 3 or 4 true leaves. Plug plants can be simply popped out of their modules; to remove seedlings sown in a tray, use the handle of a kitchen fork to gently ease out individual plants. In the first 60cm row, evenly space out 2 kale, plant each in a small hole and firm in. Plant a second 60cm row, 30cm away from the first, with 4 chard, and in the final row plant 6 perpetual spinach. Water in wet. (See illustration on page 127.)

4. The plants will eventually grow large and fill the space, but while they are still small you can make use of the space in between by sowing a row of radishes or salad leaves.
5. Allow the plants to grow for 6–8 weeks before you start harvesting. Simply pick the leaves from the outside, leaving the middle ones to carry on growing.
6. These plants are attractive to slugs and snails, and the kales are a particular favourite of caterpillars. To prevent caterpillars you will need to net your plants, which is something I should do but don't, instead choosing to remove the caterpillars by hand and take my chances. My plants can get quite badly eaten at some points in the year, but I find caterpillars to be seasonal and the plants usually bounce back. Once these plants are large, they are pretty resilient to most pests.
7. Mulch in autumn, by adding a layer of organic matter such as compost or leaf mould around the base of your plants.
8. In the second spring the plants will usually go to seed, with the kales producing side shoots that look like little broccoli. Don't waste these, as they are a fantastic spring treat – pick them and use them as you would sprouting broccoli. The more you pick the more they produce. You can also let them flower, which is great for wildlife. For the chard and perpetual spinach, break off the flower stem to prolong leaf production.
9. In mid- to late spring, remove the plants and get your new batch into the ground.

HOW TO EAT THEM: ANY GREENS PASTA

As the name suggests, this works with any greens, but I think chard and perpetual spinach are my favourite. This is a comforting winter favourite for me at a time when this is some of the only produce from the garden, and the very satisfying fleshy stems of chard add an extra layer to this dish. If using other greens such as kale, discard the stems as they will be too tough.

Serves 2

>A large bowl of garden greens – chard, perpetual spinach
>4 tablespoons extra virgin olive oil
>Salt and black pepper
>200g dried spaghetti
>2 fat cloves of garlic, finely sliced
>3 anchovy fillets
>1 small red chilli, or a pinch of dried chilli flakes
>Hearty gratings of Parmesan

Wash the green leaves and strip from the stems. Finely slice the stems and pop into a large frying pan with a couple of tablespoons of olive oil, season with salt and cook slowly for 10–15 minutes, while you cook the pasta.

Cook the pasta as per the packet instructions and add the leaves of your greens to the cooking water for the last 3 or 4 minutes.

Once softened, remove the stems from your frying pan and put them into a bowl. Add the remaining olive oil to the pan, then add the garlic, anchovy fillets and chilli. Cook on a medium heat, until the garlic goes crispy, but be careful not to burn it.

When the pasta and greens are cooked, drain, reserving ⅓ of a cup of pasta water. Add the pasta and greens to the garlic, anchovy and chilli oil, along with the pasta water and the cooked chard stems if using. Season generously with salt and pepper and serve with plenty of Parmesan.

PROJECT: GROW A RAINBOW MANGETOUT TOWER

Of all the peas, mangetout give you the most bang for your buck, because you can eat the whole pod and can harvest them the soonest after planting. However, this method also works for standard peas if you'd rather grow those. Both mangetout and shelling peas come in a range of different-coloured pods, some of which have stunningly ornamental flowers.

When to do it:
You can start seeds in a tray in mid-spring or sow seeds direct in late spring.

Time from planting to harvest:
10–12 weeks from seed.

You will need:
Mangetout seeds or plants (you can also do this with shelling peas)
A pot 30cm wide or more
3–5 × 1.5m bamboo canes (depending on the size of your pot)
Extra sticks/twiggy branches
Twine
Peat-free multipurpose or soil-based potting compost
Gravel or bark chips (optional)

Varieties to try:
Golden Sweet: A tasty and prolific yellow-podded variety.
Shiraz: Deep purple sweet pods.

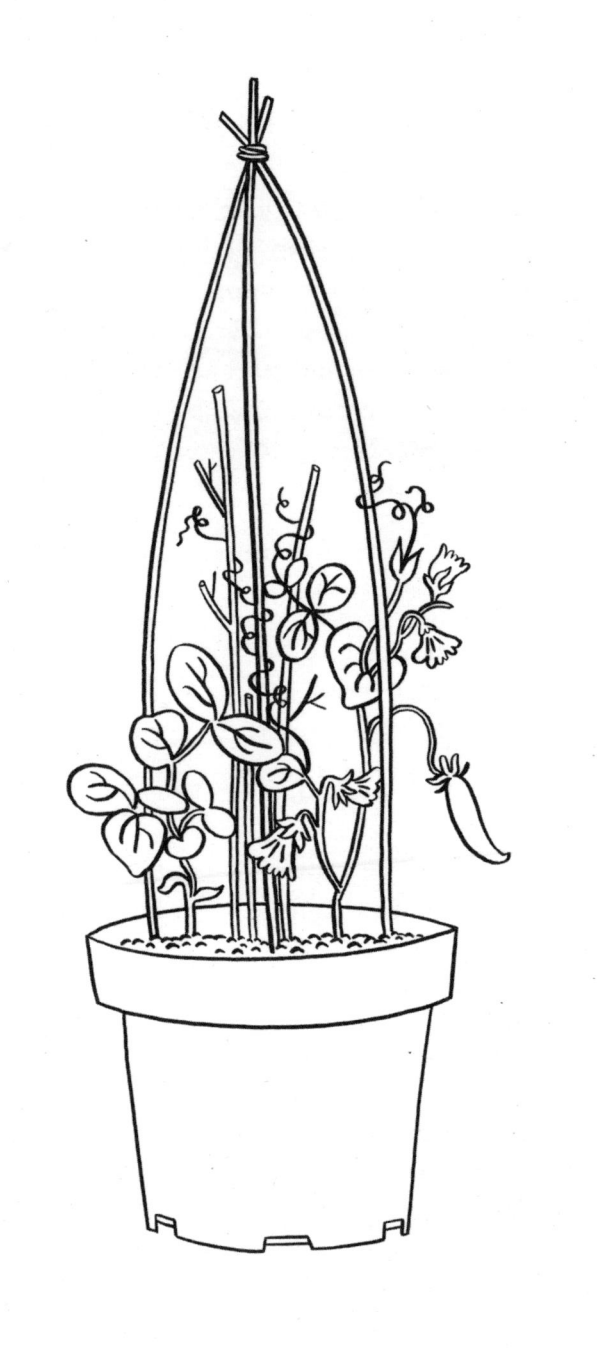

Spring Blush: Highly ornamental pink and green sugar snap peas.

Delikata: Crisp bright green pods.

How to do it:
1. You can sow the seeds direct, but I find starting seeds in a tray means you can just pop a clump of plants at the base of each support. If you plan to do the same, start your seeds 3–4 weeks before you plan to plant them in their final position.
2. To make your pea tower, first ensure that your container has drainage holes and put some drainage material in the bottom, such as broken pots or gravel. Fill with compost – a soil-based potting compost such as John Innes will give your tall pea structure more stability, but multipurpose will also work fine. Just make sure that your finished tower is out of the wind.
3. Make a structure of bamboo canes by pushing at least 3 equally spaced canes down to the bottom of your pot and tying at the top with twine. For larger containers you can build a structure with more canes.
4. Then either sow 3 seeds at the base of each cane or pop in a clump of 2–3 plants and water well.
5. Bamboo canes alone can be hard for peas to latch their little tendrils around, so I like to add a bunch of old thin sticks from my garden to the middle of the tepee, which gives them more to hold on to. Just push them down into the soil and arrange them so they spread out between the canes. Alternatively you can tie a spiral of twine around your tepee.

6. Topping with a layer of gravel or bark chips adds an attractive finish and retains moisture, but be careful not to mulch right up to the stems as this can encourage powdery mildew.
7. The peas may need tying on to the supports initially to help them find their way and stop them flopping over, but should soon climb of their own accord.
8. When your peas start to flower, feed them with a high-potassium feed (such as one formulated for tomatoes) every week to promote more flowering.
9. If growing mangetout, pick the flat pod before the peas start to fill out. They can be eaten raw or cooked. Harvest regularly to keep the plant flowering.
10. If growing shelling peas, allow the pods to swell before picking but don't leave it too long, as over-ripe peas quickly become starchy. You want to pick them when you can see the plump shape of individual peas and the pods are still glossy. They start to go dull as the peas over-ripen.
11. Fresh peas and mangetout never make it into the kitchen for me, eaten immediately on the spot. One of the best garden snacks there is.

PROJECT: CARROTS IN A CONTAINER

One of my best friends asks me to grow carrots every year because she likes pulling them up. It is true that on the scale of 'fun to harvest', carrots are at the very top, and it's really the main reason I continue to grow them. As a vegetable that is often cheap to buy and not particularly quick to grow it is not the most efficient choice, especially if you don't have a lot of space. Yet every year I plant them anyway because in my garden fun stuff sometimes trumps efficiency. Handily, carrots are well suited to container growing, as you can more readily give them the light, sandy soil conditions they desire. You can grow longer varieties of carrot in a deep bucket or pot, or if you want to make use of a shallower planter like a window box, try Chantenay, which are short, or Atlas, which are round like radishes.

You will often see trays of carrot seedlings for sale in garden centres, but carrots are best grown from seed as they don't like being transplanted. Carrot seeds also need to be kept moist to germinate well. I've found that a good solution to this is to cover seeds sown in a pot with cardboard and remove the cover when they've come up. If sowing directly into a veg patch rather than a container, a plank of wood over your sown seeds does the trick – just remember to keep checking underneath for when they pop up, and then remove the plank.

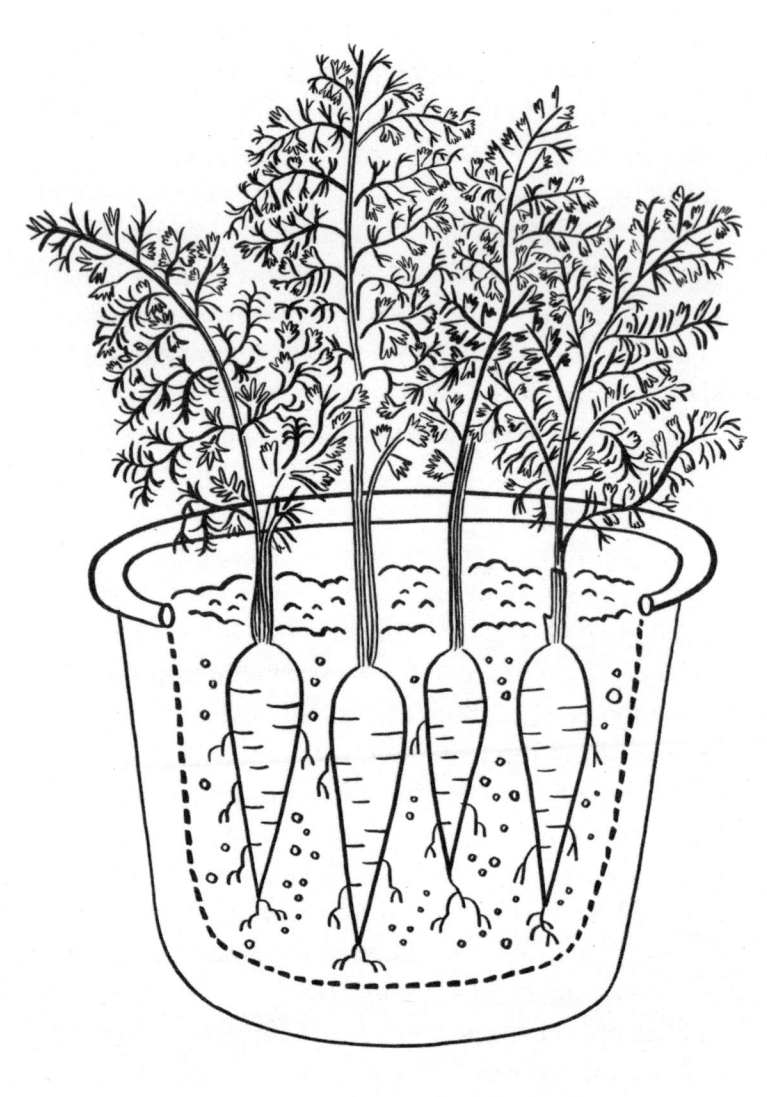

When to do it:
Mid-spring through to mid-summer.

Time from planting to harvest:
12–16 weeks.

You will need:
Carrot seeds
A container 30cm deep or more for longer carrots, or a window box for shorter varieties
Peat-free multipurpose or soil-based compost
Coarse sand (optional!)
A disc of cardboard the size of the soil surface of the pot

Varieties to try:
Atlas: Small round roots.
Chantenay: Short conical roots.
Nantes 2: Quick growing, perfect for baby carrots.

How to do it:
1. Make sure your container has drainage holes. If you have any broken pieces of terracotta, use them to cover the holes so they don't get blocked with soil.
2. Fill the container to a couple of centimetres below the top with multipurpose or soil-based compost. Those attempting to grow the longest, straightest carrots can also add a little sand to the mix, but this is not a necessary step!
3. Level the potting mix, then make a grid of holes 1cm deep and 4cm apart. Drop 2 seeds into each hole, and once you've filled all the holes, tap the pot or gently brush over the surface of the compost to fill the holes in.
4. Water gently and thoroughly, using a rose attachment on the watering can. If you just

slosh the water in, your seeds may dislodge and all collect in the same spot. Pop your circle of cardboard so that it sits inside the rim of the pot in contact with the soil, to keep it moist and aid germination.

5. Put the pot in a sunny spot and after a week start checking every few days for germination. Once the seedlings start to emerge, remove the cardboard. Carrots are susceptible to carrot root fly, and while you can cover them with horticultural fleece for protection, I take the risk, to avoid faff and keep my garden pretty. If you can put your container more than 50cm off the ground, on a table or if you are on a balcony, your crop should be safe from these low-flying critters. Keep your carrots well watered. I find it useful to use a pot saucer in my hot garden to help keep the pot moist. If both seeds from each hole germinate, thin to a single seedling.

6. If the plants become crowded, harvest alternating baby roots and be sure to eat them – they are delicious. For larger carrots, wait at least 3 months. You may see the top of the root above the soil, which is a good sign that there is something to harvest. You can always scrape back a little soil to see if there is a decent-sized carrot growing underneath, before pulling. The tops are also edible and make a good pesto.

PROJECT: POTATOES IN CONTAINERS

If there is one crop to try in a container it has to be potatoes. A must for new and seasoned gardeners alike, they are really easy to grow, don't need as much space as you might think, and there is honestly nothing more fun than tipping out a container to discover what buried treasure you've grown. You can have a go at growing potatoes from the supermarket, but seed potatoes, which are specially bred and selected for the purpose, will give you the best results, will be free of plant diseases and offer a huge range of varieties to try. You can get them online or at the garden centre from late winter through spring.

When to do it:
Mid-spring to early summer.

Time from planting to harvest:
12–20 weeks.

You will need:
Seed potatoes
A container (see below)
Peat-free multipurpose compost
Slow-release organic potato food/ blood, fish and bone or similar

Choosing your potato:
Potatoes are divided into three categories, based on how long they take to grow: first earlies, second earlies and maincrop. First earlies are the quickest to produce, taking approximately 12 weeks from planting to harvest – they take up the least space, but they also produce the lowest yield. Think of these

as 'new potatoes'. Then you have second earlies, taking about 14–16 weeks, and finally maincrop, which are the largest plants with the biggest yield and take 16–20 weeks to harvest – these are your big chipping, mashing and roasting spuds. I'm limited on space, so I usually go for first and second earlies, which can be grown in smaller containers. If you get them planted in early spring you can be eating delicious home-grown potatoes just as summer arrives.

Within the first, second and maincrop categories are a wonderful array of different potato varieties to choose from, from buttery yellow-fleshed ones, to red-skinned and even purple.

Some of my favourites are:

- **Rocket:** As the name suggests, a super quick-producing first early. A little watery in texture, so I mainly grow these for the excitement of a super early harvest.

- **Red Duke of York:** A first early with beautiful red skin and floury flesh, especially fun to dig up because of its beautiful colour.

- **Charlotte:** A much-loved second early oval potato, with rich yellow flesh perfect for boiling and covering in butter.

- **Vivaldi:** These second earlies have a large yield and make fantastic chips and röstis.

The container:
It's possible to grow potatoes in bags, bins, buckets and pots. For first earlies, a large pot or bucket is perfect. For second earlies and maincrops I'd go for a 30 litre plus container. Having said this, I'd also

encourage you to experiment, because that's all part of the fun of having a garden, and I've even had decent crops from a pot as small as 5 litres. Make sure your container has decent drainage holes.

Chitting:

This term refers to sprouting your seed potatoes before you plant them, and is commonly done with first and second earlies. The easiest way to do this is to put your potatoes into an egg box carton and leave them in a cool light place for 3–4 weeks. If you look closely, one end of your potato will have little dents called eyes where the sprouts will form, and you want this end to be facing up.

How to do it:
1. Start by filling your container 15cm deep with compost and mixing in a little organic plant food according to the packet instructions. If you have access to garden soil you can combine it with your compost to make it go further and reduce costs. Remove any large pieces and mix the compost and soil together.
2. The amount of potatoes you plant depends on the size of your container. As a rule, go for 1–2 first or second earlies in a 30cm pot or 4 in a 30 litre planter, and for maincrop 2 potatoes in a 30 litre container. Evenly space out your potatoes with the shoots or eyes facing upwards in the soil.
3. Cover the potatoes with another 10–15cm of compost mixed with a little plant food, then water. Pop into a sunny spot in your garden and leave them to sprout. Once the first green leaves appear, add another layer of compost leaving the tips of

the leaves above the soil. Repeat this as the plants grow until you reach the top of the container.
4. Potato foliage is susceptible to frost damage, so if frost is forecast, move your potatoes to a sheltered spot in a shed or indoors. They are hungry plants, so feed them every couple of weeks with an organic liquid feed.
5. It's really important to water your potatoes regularly, as the crop will be impacted if they get too dry. Bear in mind containers are susceptible to drying out, especially in warm weather.
6. Your first earlies should be ready about 12 weeks after planting, second earlies at 14–16 weeks and maincrop at 16–20 weeks. Some people say that it's time to harvest early potatoes when you see flowers, but I've never followed this rule because it's quite common for potato plants not to flower at all. I keep an eye on the calendar to remind myself how long they've been growing, and harvest when the plants start to look a little sad and start to yellow. For maincrops you can let the plants die back completely before harvesting.
7. To harvest, simply tip out your container! For less mess you can do this on to a tarp, but I'm messy and eager, so I just tip the contents out on my patio. Rummage through and find your treasure. I don't wash my potatoes until it's time to use them, as they store better with the soil on. Keep your potatoes out of sunlight, either in the fridge or in a dark cupboard, otherwise they will start to go green. I re-use the compost from my container by popping it on my garden beds, or refresh it by mixing it with about one-third

homemade compost and using it in pots to grow French beans, beetroots or carrots.

HOW TO EAT THEM: BOILED WITH ALL THE BUTTER

My favourite way to eat the very first potatoes of the year is to boil them straight away (fresh potatoes take a little less time to cook than ones from the shop). After draining, I chuck in some fresh mint, a big dollop of salty butter and an extra-large sprinkle of salt. Radishes and potatoes always arrive together in my garden, so it's a tradition to have my butter-laden spuds with crunchy fresh radishes, a few cornichons and a dollop of mayo. My perfect spring plate.

BREAKFAST RÖSTIS

For the last few years I've grown Vivaldi, which makes beautiful röstis. You want to use a potato that is good for chips/roasties, as these will go the crispiest. Second earlies are better suited to this.

Makes 6 röstis

> 5 medium potatoes, about 450g, peeled
> 1 white onion, peeled
> 1 teaspoon fine salt
> Sunflower oil, for frying

Using the larger size on your grater, grate your potatoes lengthways to produce long strands.

This will help to hold your röstis together.
Next cut the onion in half and grate it into your potatoes, discarding the root. Thoroughly mix, then add the salt and mix again. Leave for 5–10 minutes to let excess liquid be drawn out of the mix, then wrap in a tea towel and give it a good squeeze. Remove as much liquid as you can, which is usually quite a lot!

- Divide the mixture into six portions and shape into little cakes about 1–2cm thick. Take time to firm them together well, as there are no other binding agents in the recipe.
- The secret to a crispy rösti is a decent glug of sunflower oil that covers the whole base of the pan. Heat on medium-high, but make sure not to let it get so hot that it's smoking. Carefully put the röstis into the pan – they should start sizzling immediately.
- Let them start to brown and go crispy for a minute or two, then turn them over and repeat on the other side. Turn the heat down to medium and continue cooking and turning for a total of about 10 minutes, until they are beautifully medium brown, crispy and cooked through. Pop on to some kitchen paper to remove any excess oil, and sprinkle with a little more fine salt while they are still hot. My favourite accompaniments are a couple of chipolatas, some baked beans, a fried egg and some avocado.

PROJECT: GROW YOUR OWN BIG GLOSSY AUBERGINES WITHOUT A GREENHOUSE

One of the first foods I grew from seed was a miniature variety of aubergine called Bonica, which I tended to with great care, and in due course I was rewarded with just two little fruits, not much to some, but to me the most precious jewels. I have grown aubergines pretty much every year since. A strange choice perhaps for a gardener who has, until very recently, not owned a greenhouse. During a grey and wet British summer, a seed-grown aubergine is unlikely to reward you with much grown outdoors, and they will always need the sunniest spot in your garden.

But there is a solution for gardeners who have no greenhouse and still want to grow an abundance of aubergines. Buy a grafted plant (see Gardening jargon, page 35). It's something I do every year. They are not cheap and are a little tricky to come by unless bought online, but as I grow most of my plants from seed, I make special exception here since it means I can plant aubergines in the garden and harvest huge, glossy fruits that would put even those in the supermarket to shame.

When to do it:
Buy plants in late spring.

Time from planting to harvest:
Approx. 3 months.

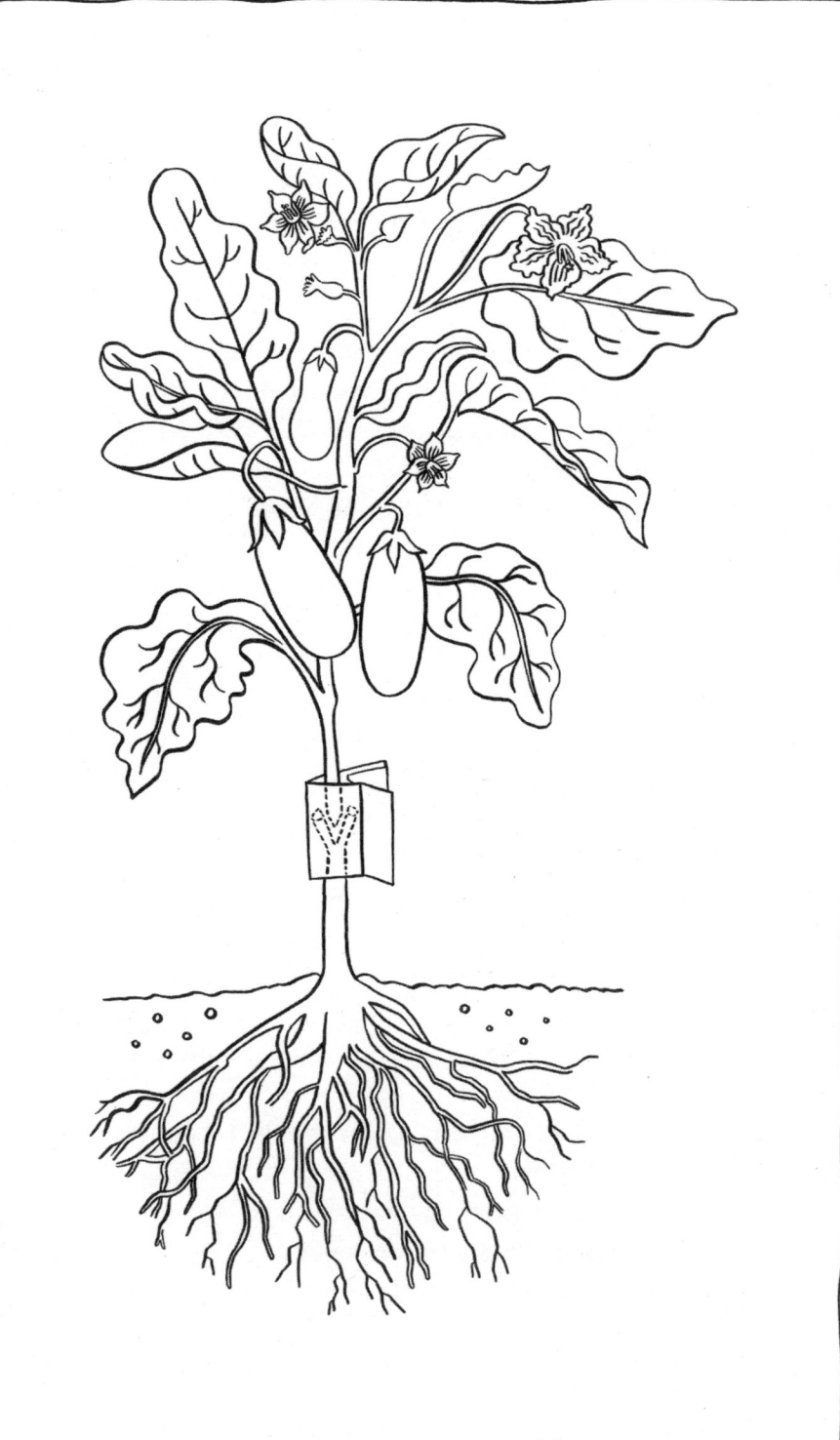

You will need:
Grafted aubergine plants (usually available as plug or potted plants)
A large pot or 30cm square patch of your veg garden, in a sunny spot

How to do it:
1. If you opt for plug plants, pot them up into small 9cm pots as soon as they arrive and keep them indoors until the weather has warmed up in late spring or early summer.
2. Remember to harden off your plants even if you've bought them in a garden centre or shop, as they may have lived most of their life in a greenhouse or protected area (see page 32).
3. Either plant them in the middle of a 30cm square patch of your prepared veg garden, or in a pot at least 30cm wide filled with peat-free multipurpose compost. Aubergines don't grow much taller than half a metre or so, but it can be useful to tie them to a short bamboo cane pushed into the ground for support.
4. I don't prune my aubergine plants, allowing them to flower and fruit as they see fit – on grafted plants I always get plenty of fruit. To get bushier plants you can pinch the tops out, or alternatively they can be grown long and tall in a cordon if you have support for them, as you would a tomato.
5. Feed plants, especially those in pots, every 1–2 weeks with an organic liquid feed high in potassium (one suitable for tomatoes is perfect).
6. Aubergines don't change colour like tomatoes or chillies as they ripen, which can make it hard to tell when they are ready. Technically they can be

eaten at any size, but as they ripen they tend to develop a more hollow sound when tapped. The most important thing is to pick them before they get over-ripe. You want to harvest aubergines when they are lovely and glossy – if they start to go dull, pick them immediately, as they are likely just past their best at this point.
7. Like chillies, aubergines are naturally perennial but will die in the cold of winter, so they are grown as annuals, with new plants started in spring.

HOW TO EAT THEM: BABA GANOUSH

In the late summer my favourite thing to do is make a big sharing platter of garden veg. Thin strips of pan-fried courgette, a bowl of tomato salad with mozzarella and basil, homemade flatbreads (page 155), which can be made without the green garlic and butter), slices of cucumber, and a bowl of the smoky aubergine dip baba ganoush.

Serves 4

2–3 large aubergines (approx. 600g)
1 large tablespoon tahini
Juice of 1 lemon
A pinch of ground cumin
½ a clove of garlic, crushed (you can use more if you like!)
A few sprigs of mint and/or parsley, finely chopped
3 tablespoons extra virgin olive oil
Salt

To get a proper smoky flavour, pop your aubergines on the barbecue or directly on the gas hob, which gives by far the best flavour. But if like me you have an induction hob, sometimes the grill just has to do even if the flavour is a lot milder. If using the grill, prick your aubergines with a fork before grilling, as otherwise they have a habit of exploding. Blacken them all over – don't worry about burning them. That is, after all, the point. When the aubergines are squishy and floppy all the way through, pop them into a bowl with a plate on top. Allow to cool, then scoop out the inside. Discard the burnt outside. Pop the flesh into a sieve and press out any excess liquid. Then finely chop.

Put the tahini into a bowl with a squeeze of lemon and mix together. If the tahini seizes up, add a little dash of warm water until it is runny again. Then add your aubergine, cumin, garlic and herbs and mix gradually, adding the olive oil. Season with the remaining lemon juice and salt to taste. You always need more lemon and salt than you think. Ideally let the dip sit for 30 minutes before eating, for the flavours to mellow and combine.

Serve with your garden platter and enjoy – a few olives and pickled chillies on the side make a great addition too.

PROJECT: GROW GARLIC GREENS ON YOUR WINDOWSILL

If you've ever found a sprouting bulb of garlic in the cupboard and wondered what to do with it, this is the answer. Let that bulb do what it wants to do – grow! Growing a full bulb of garlic from a clove takes many months, but in a few weeks you can sprout delicious garlicky shoots that are great in dipping sauces, stir-fries, or as toppings for soup. You can also do this with a bulb of garlic that hasn't sprouted, it will just take a little longer. I've tried out a few different methods for growing garlic sprouts and they all worked – at the simplest end you can just pop a whole bulb in a dish and let it sprout. I find though that leaving the skin on does make the bulb a little more likely to go mouldy.

When to do it:
All year round.

Time from planting to harvest:
2–3 weeks.

You will need:
A bulb of supermarket garlic
A small dish
A windowsill

How to do it:
1. It's worth taking the time to peel your cloves, as this keeps the garlic freshest for longest. Make sure not to cut into the cloves when doing this, and leave the base of the cloves intact, as this is where the roots will grow from.

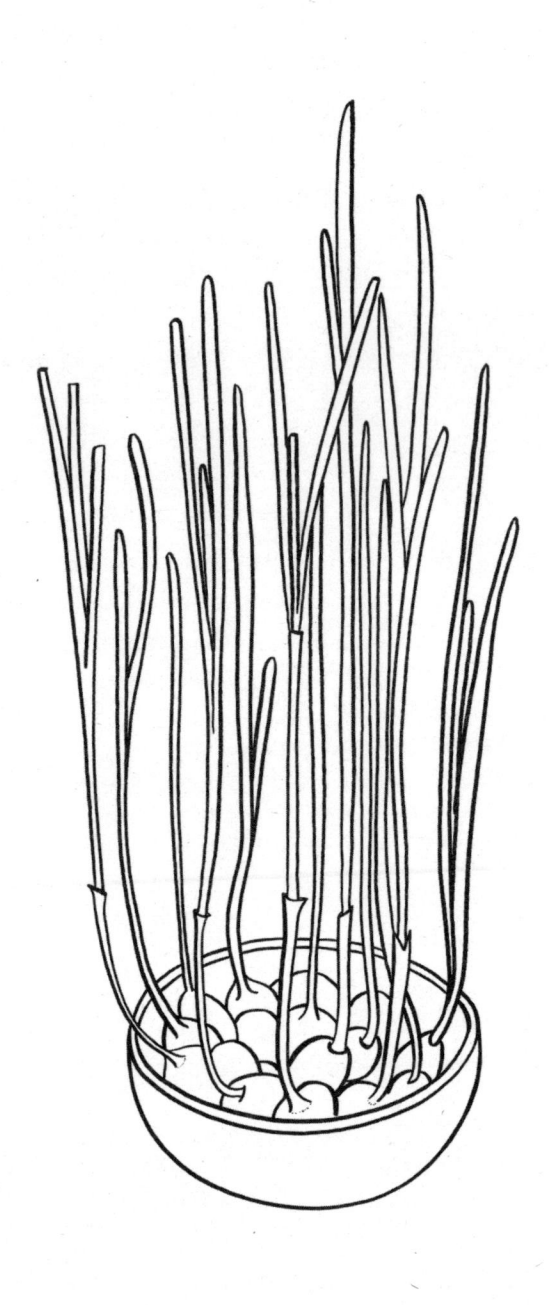

2. Arrange your cloves pointy side up in a little dish. I use 2 whole bulbs' worth of cloves so that I can neatly pack my cloves into one small bowl.
3. Add water to come about halfway up the cloves, then pop the dish on a windowsill. These don't actually need a lot of light to grow, so they can even be grown in the middle of winter.
4. Change the water every day, by carefully holding the cloves in place and pouring the water away before topping up. After a few days the roots will start to knit the cloves together, making this easier.
5. You can harvest your shoots at any size, but ideally start when they are about 15–20cm tall, which should take no more than a couple of weeks.
6. Simply snip off the green part, a couple of centimetres above the clove.
7. Your shoots will grow back several times. Eventually, after many weeks, the garlic will slow down and run out of energy, at which point it's time to compost it. If at any point it goes mouldy, which can happen, throw it out.

HOW TO EAT THEM: GARLIC FLATBREADS

Of all the things I've grown on the windowsill of my kitchen, garlic greens are the easiest and most versatile. Think of a cross between garlic and spring onion. When you cut them they release a pungent garlic smell, but when cooked they impart a much more mild and fresh garlic flavour. You can add them to pasta dishes, omelettes or make a pesto, but my favourite is to make garlic flatbreads. The beauty of this recipe is that at its most simple the flatbreads are just an equal weight of plain yoghurt and self-raising flour, so you can make as much dough or as little as you need.

Makes 4

- 3 tablespoons chopped green garlic
- 200g self-raising flour
- 200g plain natural yoghurt
- 1 tablespoon olive oil
- A pinch of salt
- 50g butter

Harvest, wash and chop your garlic greens.
Combine the flour, yoghurt, oil and salt, then knead for a few minutes to get a smooth dough.
Add half your garlic greens and knead them into the dough.
Divide the dough into four and roll each portion out on a floured surface to approximately 3mm thick.
Melt the butter in a saucepan and add the remaining green garlic. Allow to bubble in the warm butter for a minute, then remove from the heat.
Heat a medium frying pan to a high heat. Cook your flatbreads one at a time, for a few minutes on each side, until cooked through.
Brush the hot breads with the garlic butter.
Serve with whatever you fancy! I like to dunk them in a dal.

PROJECT: TURN A BAG OF LENTILS INTO WINDOWSILL MICROGREENS

Lentil greens are really easy to grow – think pea shoots but thinner and spindlier. They can rapidly grow to 20cm or so tall, so I use them as a leafy green and chuck them into recipes. They grow extremely easily – I've even grown them in a sprouting tray with just water – and once harvested they can grow back several times. A little goes a long way, and a single spoon of lentils can grow a handful of greens.

When to do it:
All year round (bear in mind very low light levels in winter can reduce growth).

Time from planting until harvest:
2–3 weeks.

You will need:
2 tablespoons dried green lentils
A container with drainage holes – a large supermarket produce container or a seed tray with holes 25 × 15cm or larger
A couple of handfuls of peat-free multipurpose compost or coconut coir
A windowsill

How to do it:
1. Put your lentils into a sieve and rinse thoroughly, then pop them into a bowl, cover with water and leave to soak overnight.
2. Next day, drain the lentils and rinse well.

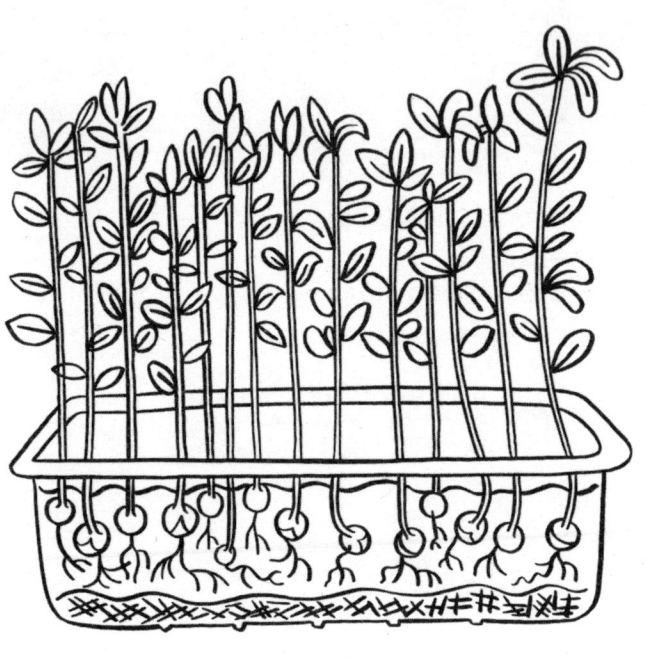

3. Take a large supermarket produce tray – if it doesn't have holes in already, make several with a pair of scissors.
4. Fill the base of your tray with 2–3cm of peat-free compost or coconut coir. Water and allow excess water to drain away. Make sure your drainage holes are working.
5. Spread the soaked lentils evenly over the surface, trying to make sure they aren't touching, as this makes them more likely to go mouldy.
6. Sprinkle another ½cm of your chosen potting mix over the top of the lentils. Firm down the soil and place on a dish.
7. Pop on to a windowsill and they should start sprouting in just a few days. Water them if the tray gets dry, but avoid over-watering.
8. Lentil greens can be eaten at any size and reach 15–20cm tall after just a couple of weeks. They also have a miraculous ability to grow back multiple times once harvested. Leave 5cm of stem when cutting them and in a week or two they'll be ready to harvest again.
9. Rinse well and they are ready to use. They can be eaten fresh like pea shoots or cooked as you would spinach.

HOW TO EAT THEM: RED LENTIL DAL

My favourite way to use lentil greens is to add them to lentils. Circle of life and all that. I make a red lentil dal with coconut milk, topped with a fried onion tarka. The greens are simply chopped up and added to the hot dal a few minutes before serving.

Serves 4–6

> 1 bunch of lentil greens, chopped

For the dal

> 400g red lentils, washed
> 1 × 400ml tin of coconut milk
> 1 large onion, chopped
> 2 medium tomatoes, chopped
> 1 small hot green or red chilli, chopped
> A thumb-size piece of ginger, grated
> 1 teaspoon ground cumin
> 1 teaspoon ground coriander
> ¼ teaspoon ground turmeric

For the tarka

> 3 tablespoons sunflower oil
> 1 teaspoon mustard seeds
> 1 teaspoon cumin seeds
> 1 large onion, finely diced

To serve

> Yoghurt or raita
> Mango chutney
> Garlic flatbreads (page 155)

Put all the ingredients for the dal into a large pot, then use the coconut milk tin to add 2 tins of water (approx. 800ml). Bring to a simmer and cook for 25–30 minutes, stirring occasionally, until the lentils are soft and losing their shape. Like a thick soup.

While the lentils are cooking, heat the oil in a small frying pan on a low heat and add the mustard and cumin seeds. Toast until the seeds start to pop – it's best to cover the pan for this! Then add the onion and cook slowly until golden brown and sweet.

Once the lentils are cooked, add the sweet onions and the lentil greens, stir to combine and allow to cook for a few more minutes.

This is delicious as is, but I like to add a dollop of yoghurt and a little mango chutney, and scoop up the dal with garlic flatbreads.

PROJECT: MAKE A SUCCESSIONAL VEG POT

A pot can be a mini veg garden all of its own, and just like a garden, you can fit much more than one plant in it across a year. Planting one crop after another can seem daunting, but follow this plan and you'll be growing all year round in no time. You can also use this same plan for a patch of your veg bed.

When to do it:
Can be started at any of the replanting/sowing stages, but starting in early spring will allow you to grow them all!

You will need:
A large pot or bucket ideally 40cm in diameter
Peat-free multipurpose compost
Drainage material

You will need these plants across the year but not all at once:

Early spring
Spinach or lettuce seeds/plants

Early summer
2 tomato plants – hanging basket or cherry indeterminate
Basil (optional)

Autumn
Garlic cloves

How to do it:

SPRING

1. Make sure your pot has good drainage holes and fill the base with some broken pots or gravel to stop the holes getting blocked with soil or roots. Fill the pot with multipurpose compost.
2. In early to mid-spring, sow your first seeds: make a series of 1cm holes with your finger in a grid pattern 3cm apart and sow each hole with either spinach or lettuce, depending on which you prefer. Both are cold-tolerant and can be picked several times. Cover the seeds over and water in. Keep an eye out for slugs and snails, as your seedlings will be especially vulnerable when they first come up. These leaves are sown very densely to produce the maximum amount of small salad leaves in the space available.
3. Your first leaves will be ready to harvest in about 6 weeks. To keep the plants producing, don't pull them up, simply pick the leaves from the outside, leaving just a few in the centre to regrow.
4. If you want to grow your own tomatoes from seed to go in your container in the summer, mid-spring is the time to get them started (follow the instructions on page 79).

SUMMER

5. In early summer, remove your spinach or lettuce plants and eat any remaining leaves.
6. Time to use the tomato plants you've grown, or buy a couple from the shops (they are widely available in late spring and early summer).

7. If you want to plant hanging basket tomatoes, these will cascade over the sides of the pot and will not need any pruning or staking. The plants tend to produce one main harvest of tomatoes. Good options are Tumbling Tom, Hundreds and Thousands and Lizzano.
8. Alternatively, you can grow 2 vining tomato varieties that will need support, giving you tomatoes over a longer period. Push 2 canes into your pot and tie them at the top to provide support for your plants. Sungold and Gardener's Delight are my favourite options for this; both are quick-ripening cherry tomatoes that are widely available as plants from the garden centre in spring and early summer.
9. If opting for vertical tomatoes grown up canes, you can add basil plants between your tomatoes. For hanging basket varieties leave the pot edges empty for the plant to spread out.
10. Feed your tomatoes every 1–2 weeks once they start flowering, using a high-potassium liquid feed. Prune vining tomatoes as described on page 87.
11. If you've planted basil, pick it as and when you need it. Pinch the tips out to harvest, as this will encourage side shoots.

AUTUMN

12. Tomatoes can continue to produce through to mid-autumn, and then it's time to remove them. Basil also won't survive a UK winter.
13. Your pot will need a little refresh after a summer growing all those tomatoes, so tip out the compost on to a patio or tarp and add one-third

of the amount of fresh compost. If you have any grit or perlite, add a couple of handfuls – this will improve drainage for your overwintering garlic, but isn't essential.

14. When growing garlic it is best to buy bulbs specially bred for growing, from the garden centre or online. Divide your garlic into cloves. Lay them out on the surface of the soil with one in the middle, then moving out in a circle, spacing the cloves 10cm apart. I usually fit 8 into a 40cm container, 7 spaced out around the outside and one in the middle.
15. Plant your garlic by pushing it pointy side upwards into the pot so the top sits 1–2cm below the surface of the soil, and water it in. You should see green shoots starting to come up after a few weeks.

WINTER AND BEYOND

16. Your garlic won't need much attention over the winter. It doesn't like sitting in the damp, so if you can raise your container off the ground with some pot feet, or put it against a wall, this will help ensure that it doesn't get too wet.
17. In the spring, feed your garlic with an all-purpose organic plant food, ideally one high in nitrogen.
18. Your garlic will be ready to harvest in mid-summer. When the leaves start to yellow, pull up the bulbs. You can use them straight away, but if you want to store them you will need to dry them. Lay them out in the sun for a few days, then hang them somewhere dry until you need them. They will keep for several months.

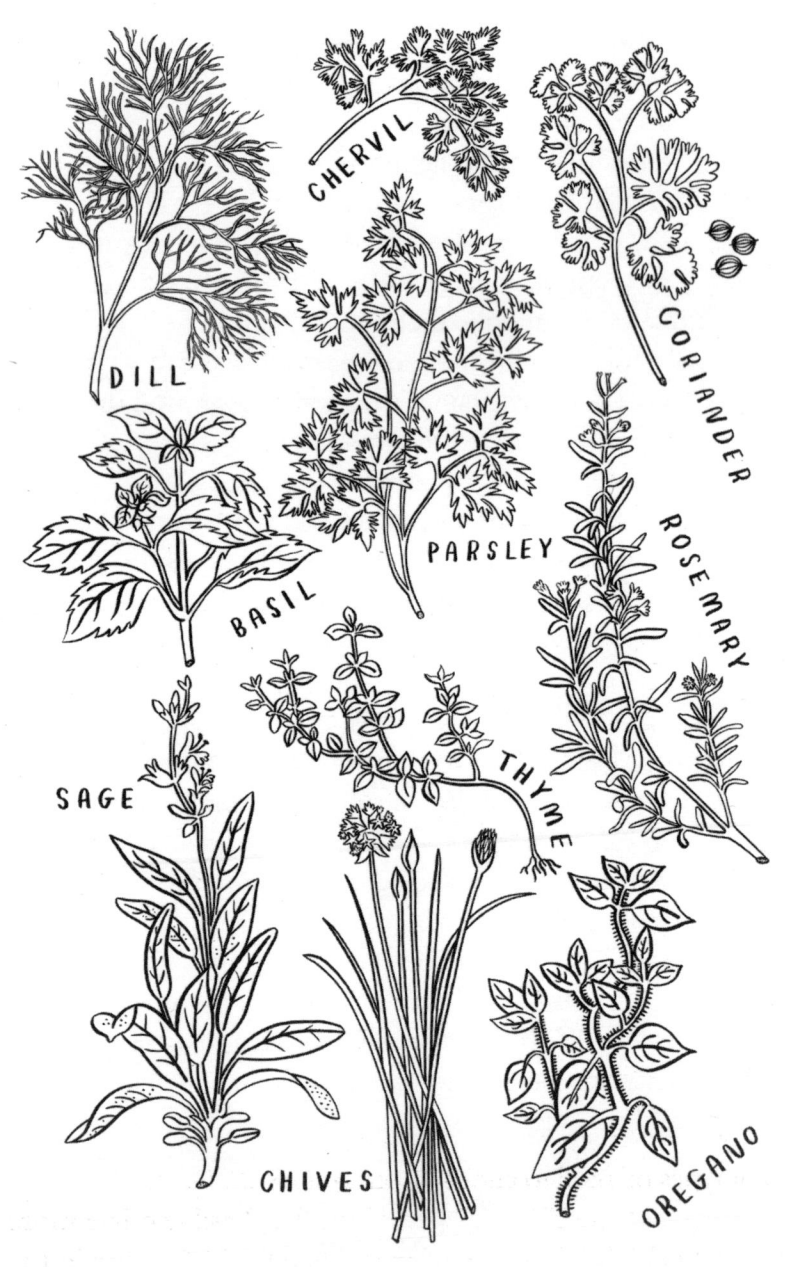

4

HOW TO GROW HERBS

Herbs are some of the most useful edible plants to have on tap, and a great entry point into growing your own food. This is not an exhaustive list of all the herbs you can grow, but more a few fun and easy projects to give you a bit of inspiration, whether you want to grow a pot of mint from leftover stems from the supermarket or plant a whole Mediterranean herb garden.

I think the most useful thing to know about herbs is which ones you can expect to live for a long time and which ones will need to be replaced every year. When coriander goes to seed and dies, it isn't your fault, it's just what the plant does. Rosemary, on the other hand, can live for many years. It just seems to be the way that the herbs we use the most are the ones that need to be resown, and those you only need a little of at a time happily live for years!

Short-lived herbs

Usually live for a year or less and need to be resown annually or multiple times a year.

Basil: A tender, heat-loving herb, there are loads of different types of basil to choose from and it's widely used in many cuisines. Depending on where you live, basil can live more than a year, but in cooler climates like the UK it dies in the winter and needs to be sown again each spring.

Chervil: A delicious relative of parsley that isn't as common as it should be. It has a lovely aniseed flavour that goes excellently with seafood and tomatoes.

Coriander: A lush aromatic herb widely used in Asian and Middle Eastern cooking, coriander needs to be sown regularly as it rapidly goes to seed, especially in the heat. You can also save and use the aromatic seeds.

Dill: An elegant, aniseed-flavoured herb, dill is especially good with fish and seafood. Start it in the spring, like coriander, but you may want to do a couple of successional sowings as it does go to seed.

Parsley: A super useful and hardy herb, parsley has a two-year life cycle, flowering in the second year. It can grow to quite a size and can be harvested for considerably longer than shorter-lived herbs like coriander, making it a fantastic herb to grow.

Long-lived (perennial) herbs

These can live for several, if not many, years.

Chives: A member of the onion family, chives is one of the few soft green herbs that live for many years. Chives also produces gorgeous miniature purple allium pom-pom flowers, which are great sprinkled on those first new potatoes of the year.

Mint: So easy to grow, it needs to be contained to stop it spreading across the whole garden. A great ingredient for adding freshness to dishes, it's also perfect for making tea.

Oregano: Possibly the easiest herb to grow that there is – bung a small plant in and you'll be rewarded with a big sprawling, scented beast. I certainly have more oregano than I can ever work out what to do with. I think I'll have to start drying it and giving it as a Christmas present.

Rosemary: A Mediterranean herb that can grow to a considerable size and provides great foraging for bees. It's easy to propagate more plants, and like many Mediterranean plants it loves sun and good drainage.

Sage: With its attractive grey foliage, sage is a very ornamental Mediterranean herb that's easy to grow and can rapidly fill out a space.

Tarragon: A delicious aniseed-flavoured herb, tarragon comes in two varieties: Russian, which is easier to grow, and French, which has a far superior flavour. French tarragon, unlike Russian, isn't hardy, so it needs to be moved to a frost-free location over winter.

Thyme: Thyme comes in lots of varieties and brings a gorgeous scent to the garden. It can be a little unhappy in British winters, but if you grow it in a pot you can move it out of the worst of the weather.

PROJECT: GROW MINT FROM THE SUPERMARKET

The easiest and most rewarding supermarket plant hack of all has to be growing your own mint. One packet of cut mint is enough to keep you in mint for the rest of time. There are a few reasons why mint is so well suited to growing from a supermarket cutting. First, you only really need the stems or the bit you usually throw away. So next time you buy mint to make a recipe or for fresh tea, you can still use the majority of the leaves before trying out this project. Second, mint grows roots really easily, so it's a great one for beginners, and the resulting plants also grow really fast. Finally, it's a perennial, which means that it will live for years, unlike many soft herbs that are just for a single season.

When to do it:
All year round, but spring is best.

Time from planting to harvest:
Allow 6–8 weeks for your plants to establish before harvesting.

You will need:
A packet/bunch of cut mint from the supermarket
A water glass
A 20cm garden pot or larger
Peat-free multipurpose compost or soil-based compost

How to do it:
1. First remove the majority of your mint leaves from the stems by simply pinching them off.

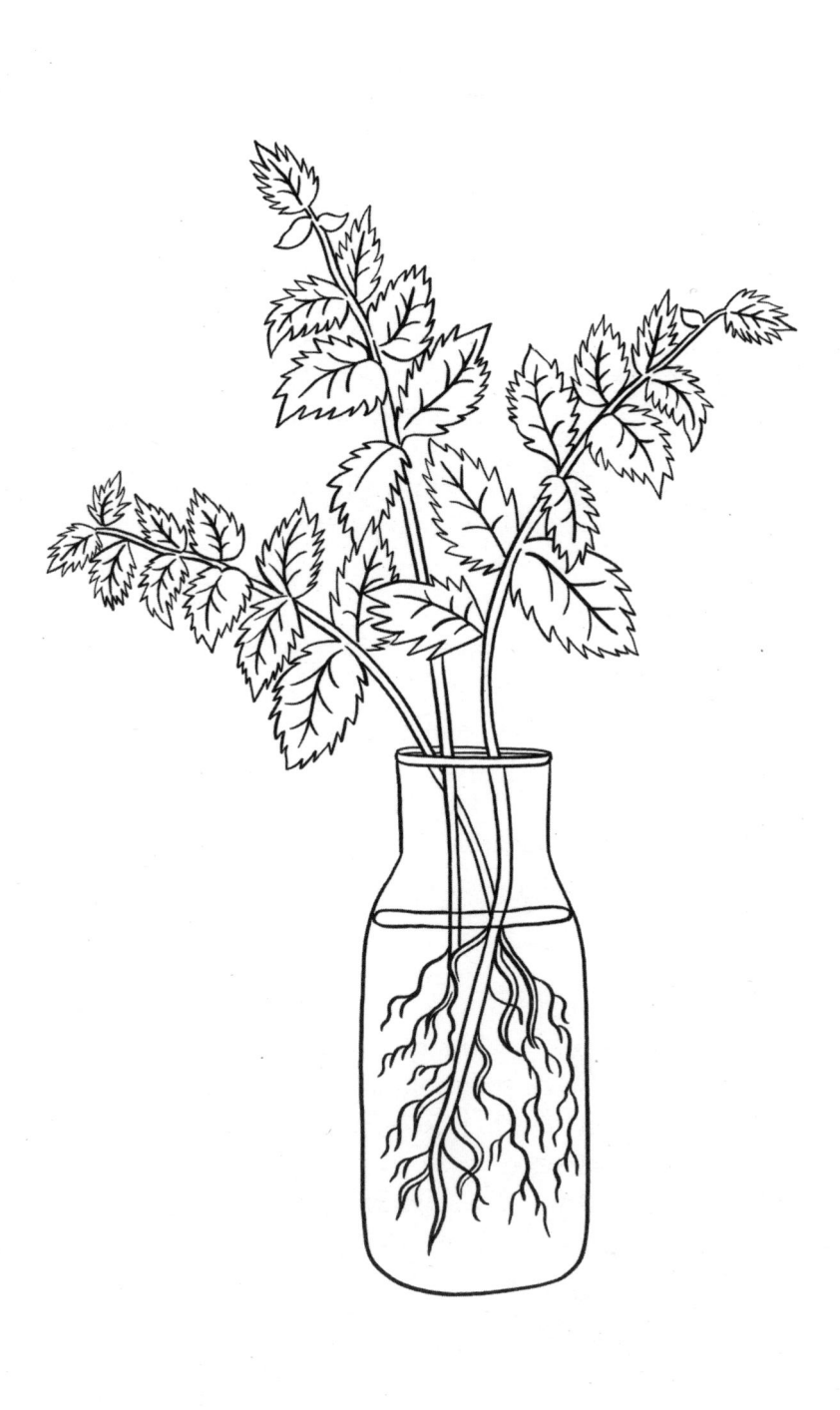

Leave just a couple of the leaves at the tip of each stem.
2. Trim the bottom of your stems, so they are freshly cut, then pop them into a glass of water with at least 5cm of the stem submerged. New roots form from the point where the leaves were removed, so make sure at least some of these points are under water. Make sure there are no leaves sitting in the water, as they can easily rot.
3. Pop the glass on a windowsill and keep the water topped up until you see roots appearing, which shouldn't take more than a couple of weeks.
4. Once you have roots on your mint it's time to pot up your little plants. Now, a very important thing to note about mint is that it is incredibly invasive. That means if you put it directly in the ground in your garden it will spread all over the place. It produces long horizontal underground stems from which new shoots of mint will spring up all over your garden. It's then very difficult to remove. As a result, it's much better to grow mint in a pot, where it can be contained.
5. Take your pot, ensuring it has a drainage hole, and fill it with multipurpose or soil-based compost. Make 3–5 holes in the soil and pop a bit of rooted stem into each. Firm the soil back around the stem.
6. Once your plants are growing away, which will take about 6 weeks, you can harvest them whenever you need to. The best way to do this is by pinching out the leaves at the top of a stem rather than taking individual leaves off the side. Pinching out the tip will encourage the plant to

grow new shoots all along the stem and make bushier plants.
7. Mint pretty much looks after itself, but you may notice the plants looking tired towards the end of the summer, when they may start to flower. The best thing to do is cut back the mint to the surface of the soil, top up with a little more fresh compost, give it a good water, and after a few weeks new leaves will appear.
8. Mint is cold-tolerant and can be left outside over winter, ideally in a sheltered spot. The leaves may be damaged by frost, and the plant may disappear completely over the winter, but it will return with new growth in the spring.

PROJECT: GROW LEMONGRASS FROM THE SUPERMARKET

Lemongrass, as the name suggests, is a type of grass with a gorgeous lemon scent. With a little encouragement, supermarket lemongrass will happily grow into a clump of fragrant stems and leaves which you can use to cook with, or just trim off a leaf or two to make a fragrant lemony tea. Lemongrass is a tropical plant, so while it's happy outside during the summer months, it will need to be brought inside for the winter before night-time temperatures fall below 5°C.

When to do it:
Lemongrass can't survive the cold, so the best time to do this is early spring. It can take up to a month for the stems to sprout, so start them in mid-spring, ready to put outside in early summer.

Time from planting to harvest:
You can harvest leaves a couple of months after planting; stems can take 6 months or more.

You will need:
4 lemongrass stems
A water glass
Peat-free multipurpose compost
A 30cm pot

How to do it:
1. It's possible to sprout lemongrass from just the bottom few centimetres of a stem, if you are keen to experiment with using up leftover scraps. However, I've had the best success using the

whole stem. Simply pop your lemongrass stems into a fresh glass of water so that at least 5cm is submerged, and wait for them to grow roots. Keep the water topped up and change it once a week. It can take 3–4 weeks for roots to appear, so don't give up! It's worth doing 4 or more stems at a time so you can fill up a pot with your plants.
2. Once they have roots, it's time to pot up your plants. Fill your pot with peat-free compost, then pop in your stems, spacing them out evenly in the pot. Water in well.
3. Let your plants grow on a sunny windowsill, or gradually acclimatize them outside if all risk of frost has passed.
4. As the lemongrass grows it will produce new stems from the base of each plant, forming a clump over time. The part used for cooking is the swollen bottom part of the stem, which may take some time to grow to size, but the leaves are also extremely fragrant and just a few weeks after potting up can be harvested to make fresh tea. Simply snip them off as and when you need them.
5. Once your plant is established, you can harvest lemongrass whenever you want. You're looking for the largest swollen stems that are 2cm or more thick. Using a sharp knife, carefully cut the base of the stem as far down as possible, trying not to damage any thinner immature stems either side.
6. Lemongrass is a tender plant that cannot be left out when night-time temperatures fall below 5°c. You can grow lemongrass as an annual and harvest it all in autumn, but I find it takes

a couple of years in the cooler, UK climate for plants to grow to decent size, so I prefer to treat mine as a perennial and bring it indoors over winter. Harvest any larger stems, then trim the remaining thinner stems down to 10cm. Pop your lemongrass on to a bright windowsill, ideally in a cool location away from central heating. An unheated greenhouse will not be warm enough for lemongrass over the winter in the UK. Water lightly and regularly to stop the plants drying out in the heat of your home.

7. In late spring the plants can be hardened off and put back outside for the summer, when the night-time temperatures are safely above 5°c and all risk of frost has passed. Lemongrass can live for many years and forms large clumps over time, which can be split up and repotted to make new plants.

PROJECT: GROW ROSEMARY FROM A CUTTING

Like many plants, a new rosemary plant can be grown from just a small piece of a larger bush. This is known as a cutting, and it's a great way to create free plants in your garden. If you have a friend who already has a rosemary plant, you can use this method to grow a whole new one for free. You rarely see rosemary seed, because it takes ages to grow and cuttings are much quicker. You can even do this with a packet of cut rosemary from the supermarket, but fresh cuttings will give you the best chance of success. Cuttings are a great way to grow new, free plants and you can use this method for loads of plants including mint, lavender and sage, as well as lots of wildlife-friendly perennial flowers.

When to do it:
Rosemary is best propagated in spring or autumn.

Time from planting to harvest:
It may take several months or longer for your rosemary cutting to develop into a small plant, but it will live for many years.

You will need:
Several fresh cuttings of rosemary (around 15cm long)
A small square pot
Peat-free multipurpose compost
Grit or perlite

How to do it:
1. You can have a go at taking cuttings of rosemary throughout the growing season, but for the best

chances of success either take cuttings of the fresh growth in spring (softwood), or cuttings of the same year's growth that is starting to turn woody in autumn (semi-ripe). Simply snip off a 10–15cm length, below a set of leaves. Make sure to take several cuttings in case some don't work.
2. Don't let your cuttings dry out. Remove the lower leaves and either pop your cuttings into a glass of water and leave them to root before potting them up, or put them straight into a mix of 50% compost and 50% grit or perlite, pushing the stems down into the corners of a square 9cm pot, 4 cuttings per pot. Water well.
3. Covering your pot with a large sandwich bag will help keep moisture in and give your cuttings the best chance of rooting sucessfully. Keep in a well-lit, sheltered spot out of direct sunlight.
4. After a month or two, gently take the cuttings out of the pot in one clump. Ease the separate plants apart and pot up individually.
5. For water-rooted cuttings, pot them up into individual pots once they have roots. Grow them on until the plants are established and have formed a good root system – check if you can see roots through the holes in the bottom of the pot.
6. They are now ready to go into their final location. Rosemary is a Mediterranean herb that loves good drainage and plenty of sun. It can be planted in a container on its own or with other herbs, or direct in the garden in a sunny spot.

PROJECT: GROW A CONSTANT SUPPLY OF CORIANDER

Coriander is, in my opinion, a herb you can never have too much of. But you either love it or you hate it, given that a genetic quirk means that to some people it just tastes like soap. It's a short-lived plant, quickly going to seed, so the secret of having a constant supply is to keep sowing it. The flowers are edible, and if you are willing to wait you can also harvest the edible seeds. The plants last longest in the cooler months of spring and autumn, rapidly going to seed in the heat of the summer.

When to do it:
Mid-spring to mid-autumn.

Time from planting to harvest:
Approx. 6 weeks.

You will need:
Coriander seeds
Two 20cm pots or larger
Peat-free multipurpose compost

How to do it:
1. Start with one pot, fill it with your compost, and sprinkle the coriander seeds over the surface. Cover with 1cm of soil and water in gently – if you slosh a load of water in, your seeds will float around and come up patchy. Although coriander can tolerate some shade, it will do best in a sunny spot. Keep well watered. The seeds can take a while to germinate, so don't despair!

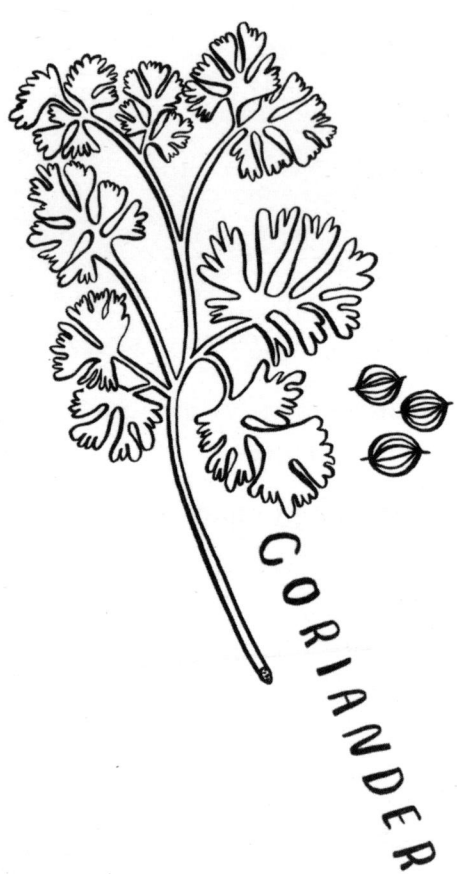

2. After about 6 weeks, sow your second pot in the same way as the first.
3. As your seedlings come up, you may find the pot is rather crowded, in which case thin out by gently removing whole plants once they have their first true leaves. These make an excellent garnish. Harvest larger plants by cutting off leaves as and when you need them, leaving the plants to regrow.
4. Harvest coriander from your first pot until it starts to produce a flowering stem. At this point you have a choice to make: you can remove and use what's left of the plants and resow your next batch of coriander, or simply allow the plant to flower and use the edible blooms to decorate dishes, or leave them to form seeds which you can collect and dry to use in cooking. In the meantime you can start harvesting your second pot of coriander.
5. Coriander grows best in the cooler spring and autumn months and can survive fairly well into the winter, especially if you are able to give it some protection in a cold frame or greenhouse.

PROJECT: GIVE SUPERMARKET PARSLEY A NEW LEASE OF LIFE

Many potted supermarket herbs like parsley are sown thickly, and rarely with a view to living a long time. But you can change all that. Take home a pot of parsley and give those tightly packed plants a new lease of life in a container in your garden. You can also do the same with basil, of which I have several happy plants in my garden, all from a single small supermarket pot. I learned this trick from my mum, who always has an abundance of parsley in the garden which she grows from supermarket plants.

When to do it:
Spring or summer – wait until it's warm to plant supermarket herbs outdoors, as they could get a shock if the weather is cold.

Time from planting to harvest:
Allow your plants a month or so to establish before starting to harvest.

You will need:
A pot of parsley from the supermarket (make sure it's not come from the fridge, and choose a sturdy, healthy-looking plant if possible)
A medium-sized pot
Peat-free multipurpose compost
A bowl of water

How to do it:
1. If your plant has any especially tall or floppy leaves, start by cutting these off, leaving just the

smaller, newer shoots. This will reduce evaporation from your little plants and give them time to establish better. Use your trimmings in a recipe!
2. Take your parsley out of its pot and place it in a bowl of water.
3. If you look closely, you will see that the clump is made up of lots of individual plants. Gently tease the plants apart, trying to avoid breaking the roots as much as possible.
4. Fill your pot with compost and spread out your parsley plants, leaving 5cm between plants, making a hole for each plant and dropping it in, so that it sits at the same level that it was previously planted.
5. Firm in and water well. You can also pop these little plants into any gaps in the garden, for example around the edge of planters next to larger plants.
6. Once your parsley is established and happily growing you can start to harvest it a little at a time.
7. Parsley is a biennial plant, meaning that it lives over a two-year period. It often survives the winter and will start to go to seed in the spring, when it's time to replace it.

PROJECT: MAKE A CONTAINER HERB GARDEN

A great way to get started growing your own food is to make a herb garden in a container. It also makes a lovely gift and is a great project to do with kids. Of all the things from the supermarket that get wasted, half-used packets of herbs have to be right up there, and growing a selection of your own means you can harvest just what you need when you need it, adding a little home-grown goodness to every meal. For the greatest chance of success, use quality plants from the garden centre, but if you are up for a bit of experimenting, cheaper plants from the supermarket can go on to have a happy second life in the garden.

If you have space for a couple of planters, it's a good idea to group herbs together that like similar conditions. Parsley, coriander, basil and chives all enjoy rich, moist and well-drained soil and can cope with a little light shade. Thyme, sage and rosemary are all perennial Mediterranean herbs, so they thrive in really well-drained soil in lots of sun and with a bit of care can live for several years. If you plant a mix of long- and short-lived herbs, you can either let the longer-lived herbs grow into the gaps left after the shorter-lived ones have ended, or plant new tender or short-lived herbs like basil and coriander each year. Mint is best planted in a pot on its own, as it spreads very quickly.

When to do it:
Spring/summer.

You will need:
A selection of your favourite herbs
A large container, such as a window box, metal trough or large terracotta pot
Soil-based or peat-free multipurpose compost
Grit or perlite
Drainage material
Gravel for decoration (optional)

How to do it:
1. If adapting a container such as a metal trough, you will need to make drainage holes. The easiest method is to use a drill with the appropriate drill bit – holes 1cm or larger are less likely to get clogged.
2. Fill the base of the container with drainage material, such as broken pots or broken crockery.
3. If growing Mediterranean herbs such as thyme, rosemary and sage, it's especially important to add extra drainage to your potting mix, so combine a third of grit or perlite with your compost.
4. Give your plants a good watering before potting them up, especially if they are dry.
5. Fill your planter about two-thirds full with your potting mix. Arrange your herbs in the container, leaving space for your plants to grow, and fill back around the plants with the remaining potting mix. If you are using herbs from the supermarket, bear in mind that they sow these very thickly, especially basil, parsley and coriander, so divide these plants into four pieces and plant them with a gap between clumps. Water your plants in well.

6. For an attractive finish, dress the top of the container with gravel, which will also help retain some moisture.
7. Put your planter in a sunny spot, especially if you've chosen sun-loving Mediterranean herbs.
8. Harvest as and when you need. Herbs are best harvested by moving the tips, rather than individual leaves, as this will promote side shoots.
9. In the winter your annual herbs will die and will need to be resown in the spring. Perennials will usually survive the winter without protection in milder areas, but they don't like to sit in wet soil. Popping your container against a wall and ideally raised off the ground will help keep your plants happy in the winter.

PROJECT: GROW A MEDITERRANEAN HERB GRAVEL GARDEN

In the centre of my garden is a gravel patio. When I built it, I removed the lumpy old lawn and topped the soil with builders' sand and hessian fabric instead of using plastic weed sheets. While the hessian rapidly breaks down, I rarely get weeds growing up through my gravel, and if I do they are easy to remove.

What I love about my gravel area is that I can put plants around the edges. The gravel both retains heat and reflects light, making it perfect for sun-loving Mediterranean herbs (both my lavender and my oregano have absolutely thrived). They are happy to grow in fairly poor soil, and as long as there is good drainage they can just be popped into the soil without any amendments. You could also use this method to create a fragrant herb border along a gravel pathway.

When to do it:
From spring to early autumn, but avoid planting in very hot weather.

You will need:
Mediterranean herbs such as rosemary, lavender, sage, thyme, marjoram
Sunny gravelled area to plant them, which has soil underneath

How to do it:
1. Lay out your potted herbs on the gravel to create the desired effect. Put thyme in front of plants like rosemary and lavender which grow

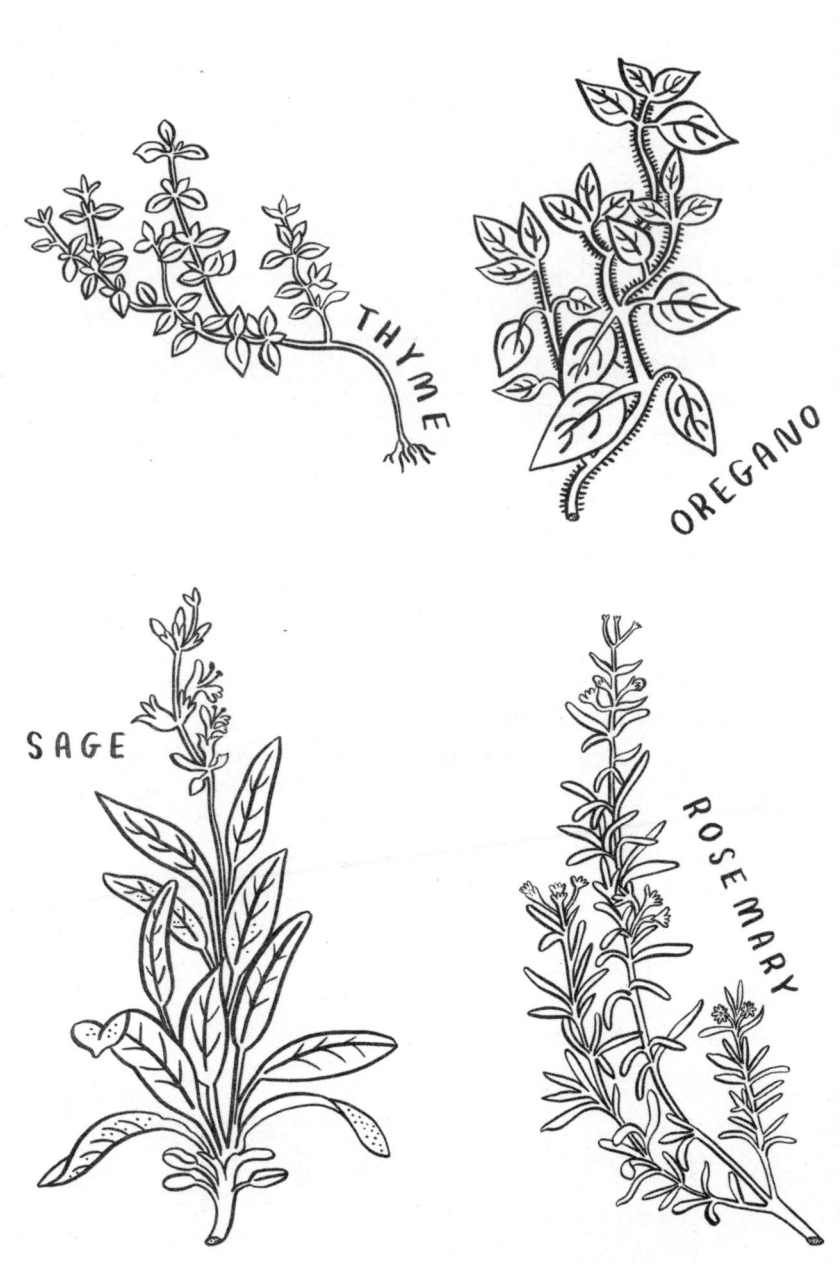

rapidly – thyme doesn't cope well with shade and if overshadowed could die.
2. Bear in mind that small potted herbs can rapidly expand, especially oregano, which is now 60cm wide in my garden, so leave a 30cm gap between your plants.
3. Scrape back the gravel in your desired planting spot and dig a hole the same size as the pot.
4. Water your plants well before planting out, and tease the roots if they are rootbound.
5. Pop your herbs into their holes, firm them in, and bring the gravel back around the base of the plant. Water well.
6. Keep your plants watered well as they establish, and especially in hot weather.
7. After the first year's growth, prune your herbs back annually to keep them compact. The best time to do this is usually after flowering.

5

HOW TO GROW FRUIT

There is a fruit for every size of garden or outdoor space, from strawberries to apples, pears and even citrus. Home-grown fruit is delicious, and there is definitely something luxurious about wandering around your garden picking berries straight off the plant. Fruit is often a long game, with trees and bushes taking a couple of years or more to start producing, but once planted they need only a little maintenance to get a harvest every year. And for those of us who are impatient, there are fruits that you can pick the same year. A bonus of fruit trees is the beautiful display of blossom in spring, buzzing with bees, and I think a tower of strawberries dripping with ripe fruit is as ornamental as any floral display.

STRAWBERRIES

Very few things are as fun to pick straight from the garden and devour as fresh strawberries, especially those warmed by the sun on a glorious summer's day. Strawberries are perfect for growing in small gardens, as they are extremely well suited to container growing. They are also perennial, meaning that they will live and produce strawberries for multiple years. An extra bonus is that they produce new plants every year on long shoots that they send out in the summer, which means that once you've started growing strawberries you can have a steady supply of fresh plants to expand or replace your collection as and when you need. With a little planning it's also possible to have strawberries for many months.

Choosing your strawberry

Wild strawberries: These tiny little plants spread happily in semi-shaded areas and produce miniature super-sweet berries.

Early, mid, late season: Different varieties of strawberry flower at different times. The label should tell you what type a plant is. If you get a mix, you can extend your season.

Ever bearers: Some strawberries flower continuously across a season – they will fruit less at any one time but for a longer period.

Growing strawberries

From seed
It is possible to start strawberries from seed, but the seeds are often expensive and a little temperamental. The most common varieties you will find sold as seed are wild strawberries (see page 204).

From plants

The easiest way to grow strawberries is to start with plants. You will find potted plants widely available from garden centres throughout the spring and summer. Many will already come with flowers or fruit on, which can be very appealing. I usually succumb to the allure of imminent strawberries and let the plants ripen the fruits, but if you have the will-power to remove the flowers in the first year the plants will put their energy into growth and will give you a bigger harvest next year.

I prefer to get bare-root strawberry plants in the autumn. These plants are often cheaper than getting potted ones in the spring. They are widely available online in the colder months and will arrive without soil in a bundle. They may not even have leaves, but don't be put off, strawberry plants are tough and they will soon spring into life. The benefit of planting strawberries in the autumn is that the plants can establish over winter and will be ready to give you a crop of fruit the following spring. Bare-root plants just need to have their roots soaked in water for about an hour before planting and then they are ready to go.

PROJECT: MAKE A STRAWBERRY TOWER

The perfect way to grow strawberries is along the edge of something, whether that be a raised bed, a pot, a hanging basket or even a stretch of raised guttering (a method often employed in commercial production), because then the fruit can hang over the side. This strawberry tower exposes the plants to the sun for better ripening; it makes them easier to pick and less likely to be eaten by slugs and snails than if the fruit was lying on the ground, and is most of all a great use of space.

When to do it:
Bare-root plants in autumn, potted plants in spring.

Time from planting to harvest:
If planting in autumn they will fruit the following summer; if using potted plants in spring they are likely to fruit the same year, but harvests may be small.

You will need:
10 strawberry plants, either potted or bare-root (depending on the size of the pots)
3 pots of various sizes – you can use whatever you have, but 40cm, 25cm and 12cm is a good combo
Peat-free soil-based potting compost
Drainage material

How to do it:
1. This planting tower is ideally done against a wall for stability, and in a sunny spot the wall will create a nice warm microclimate for your strawberries. Make sure your pots all have drainage holes.

2. Starting with the largest pot, cover the base with some broken pots or gravel to stop any soil clogging up the drainage holes. Fill the pot with potting mix to the top of the pot and firm the soil down.
3. Around the front side of the pot, dig a hole for each plant at 10cm intervals. You want the crown (the woody stem at the top of the roots, which is also where new shoots will emerge) to sit at the same level as the top of the soil. If planted too deeply the plants can rot. In a large 40cm pot you should be able to fit 5 plants around the front of the rim, leaving a gap at the back.
4. Now take your middle-sized pot and prepare it with gravel and compost as you did with the larger one. Plant 3 plants around the front side of the pot, then place this pot on top of the soil in the larger pot, in the space you left without plants.
5. Prepare the smallest pot with gravel and compost like the others, then finish with 2 plants and place on the top of the tower. Gently press the tower down to firm it in place, with the back of all the pots resting against the wall.
6. Dress the top of the pots around the plants with a mulch, such as gravel, and water all the pots well.
7. In the spring you will notice new growth on your strawberries. When you spot the first strawberry buds, give them a high-potassium liquid feed.
8. Protect the flowers from any late frost with some fleece. If you find flowers with dark brown centres after a cold snap, remove these

flowers – they are frost-damaged and won't produce fruit.
9. Keep your plants well watered and fed when they are flowering and fruiting. Netting will protect them from birds and squirrels. Keep an eye out and remove any slugs and snails in the vicinity, as they love munching on a strawberry.
10. Cherish your first strawberry of the season! A special treat.
11. When your plants have finished fruiting in late summer, cut back any old leaves as this will promote new growth. Don't forget to keep your plants well watered and fed throughout the rest of the growing season into autumn, to ensure they are strong and ready for next year.

PROJECT: GROW FREE STRAWBERRY PLANTS

This couldn't be easier. Strawberry plants send out long shoots called runners that are looking for new ground, and along these shoots are little baby strawberry plants, clones of their parents. In fact, strawberries grown in the ground will rapidly root their new plants themselves. This can lead to congested strawberry patches with too many plants, so it's best to move these young plants to a new location. They can easily be dug up and potted and given to friends, or you can use them to replace older plants. Runners produced from container strawberries need a little help to get growing.

When to do it:
Summer, when you see your strawberry plants producing runners.

Time from rooting to growth:
This year's runners will produce their first fruit the following year.

You will need:
Small pots (9cm is ideal, but whatever you have around – you could even use a tin can with drainage holes)
Peat-free multipurpose compost

How to do it:
1. Fill a small pot with garden soil or compost and water well, then sit it on the ground next to your container strawberry.

2. Make sure to choose runners that reach down far enough to sit comfortably in your pot.
3. Find a little plant on the runner and push it gently into the soil, root side down, just far enough so that any roots are sitting against the soil and the plant remains in place. If it won't stay put, it can be secured with a small twig bent in half, a tent peg or similar. Water the pot thoroughly.
4. After a few weeks your plant should have rooted and is ready for you to simply snip it from the stem that connects it to the main plant.
5. Strawberry plants are hardy, so these plants can be left outside over winter, ready to plant in their final location in spring, by which time they should have developed a good strong root system.

PROJECT: FILL YOUR GARDEN WITH WILD STRAWBERRIES

Wild strawberries are a miniature cousin of the much larger strawberries you find in the shops. They are much smaller plants that are more tolerant of shade than regular strawberries, and produce small, super-sweet and fragrant berries continuously for several months. These delicate little wildflowers are also popular with pollinators, so win, win all round. As a child, a family friend of ours had a garden with wild strawberries growing under a hedge – I would climb inside on the hunt for the little red gems, and I still think there's something a little magical about wild strawberries. My own little garden has wild strawberries hidden all over the place. I bought a tray of twenty plug plants online and set about bunging them in. I mostly use them as attractive edible ground cover underneath fruit trees, both in the ground and in pots. A little enchanted extra bonus crop from a space that otherwise might not be used. I like to think of it as my own little edible forest garden in miniature. Wild strawberries rapidly produce runners and will spread around your garden, which for me is part of the fun, but might not be for everyone!

When to do it:
Sow seeds in early spring.
Plant plugs or bare-root plants in autumn or spring.

Time from planting to harvest:
Sometimes seed-sown plants will fruit the same year, otherwise the following season. Plants planted in autumn will usually fruit the following spring.

HOW TO GROW FRUIT

You will need:

Wild strawberry plants (plug plants are the most cost-effective option if you don't grow from seed yourself)

A spot to plant them!

Growing from seed:

Wild strawberry plants can be harder to find than regular strawberries, so growing from seed is a cost-effective, if slightly slower, option. The seeds need light and moisture to germinate, which can take a few weeks. Best done in late winter or early spring, as they take a while to get growing.

1. Fill a pot or small seed tray with seed compost, or use multipurpose with any large bits removed. Water the soil and let any excess drain off before adding your seeds, as they are tiny and can easily be washed away.
2. Sprinkle the seeds lightly on the surface of the soil and do not cover, then pop into a propagator or inside a sealed sandwich bag (you can re-use these multiple times for starting seeds).
3. Place in a warm, light location such as a sunny windowsill, or on a heated mat if you have one.
4. Seedlings should appear in 2–4 weeks.
5. Once the seedlings have their first true leaves, pot them up into individual pots.

How to do it:

1. Once you've got your plants it's time to plant them out. If you've grown them from seed yourself they will need to be acclimatized gradually to the outdoors and planted out after

the risk of frost has passed. However, if you've bought plants these can often be planted straight out even when it's cooler.

2. A sunny or lightly shaded spot is ideal, but most importantly the spot you choose needs to be open. If your plants get engulfed by larger plants nearby they won't thrive, an easy mistake to make in winter or spring, when the garden is bare of summer growth. Under fruit trees in the ground or in a pot, along the edges of a flower bed or even in a gravel patio (see page 191) are good options. The idea is to have fun popping little plants around the place. Bear in mind that wild strawberries can rapidly spread and multiply.

3. Water your plants well before planting them out, then dig a little hole in your chosen location and pop them in. If going straight into uncultivated garden soil, add a little peat-free multipurpose compost to the potting hole to give them a good start. Leave 20cm space between plants, but remember, spacing is flexible – wider spacing gives plants more room to grow larger, but if you want to put a ring of plants around a fruit tree in a pot don't feel you have to get your tape measure out.

4. Water them in well. These plants need little maintenance. In fact, after I put mine out I forgot they were there until I noticed they'd tripled in size. Wildlife may be tempted to steal your fruit, but I find netting little plants like this too much hassle so I'm willing to share – they are after all a great plant for nature.

PROJECT: GROW TROPICAL-FLAVOURED PHYSALIS FRUIT IN A SINGLE SEASON

Lots of fruit takes a few years before you get to harvest in earnest. A big bonus of physalis or Cape gooseberry, a relative of the tomato, is that it produces fruit in the same year. These little fruits come inside a paper husk that looks like a little lantern, hiding an orange orb inside. Sometimes erring on the sharp side, they have a tropical fruity flavour. In warmer places than the UK they grow like a weed, but when I first managed to grow them in the UK I was delighted. They will grow best in a pot in a sunny spot.

From seed:
If you've grown tomatoes from seed, the process is very similar: physalis need to be started early in the year, ideally with some heat, and they can't go outside until all risk of frost has passed. Follow the instructions for growing tomato seeds on page 79. You can also increasingly often find these plants in garden centres and even large supermarkets.

When to do it:
After all risk of frost has passed, in late spring/early summer.

Time from planting to harvest:
Approx. 12 weeks.

You will need:
1 *Physalis peruviana* plant
A large pot 30cm or more wide
Drainage material

Peat-free multipurpose compost
A plant pot saucer or a plate
Mulch, such as bark chips or gravel

How to do it:
1. Make sure your container has good drainage holes and fill the bottom of the pot with gravel, rocks or clay beads. Physalis are not fussy plants but they don't want to sit in water.
2. Water your physalis well before potting it up.
3. Here is a neat trick to fit your plant perfectly into its hole. Fill your pot with peat-free multipurpose compost, about two-thirds full, then place your plant, pot and all, in the middle. Continue adding compost around the potted plant. Firm it down, then remove your plant, pot and all, take it out of its pot and pop it back into the perfect-sized planting hole you've made. If your plant is rootbound, gently tease the roots before planting.
4. Water well and top your pot with a layer of mulch. Sit your pot in a pot saucer to ensure it gets fully hydrated when you water it.
5. Keep it in a sunny warm spot, such as against a south-facing wall. In cooler areas these plants may need the protection of a greenhouse or polytunnel to fruit well.
6. They require no pruning and can be left to their own devices.
7. The plants will produce little yellow flowers that open, then close and turn into little green lanterns. They are rather charming in the garden and gradually fade to a papery husk with a round orange fruit inside. Once they start to flower

you can feed them with a high-potassium feed formulated for tomatoes, to encourage the fruits to develop.
8. Fruit is ripe when the papery husk fades from green to a pale straw colour and the fruit inside has turned bright orange. Ripe fruit may fall from the bush but is often protected by the husk and is still good to eat, if not sweeter than fruits picked from the plant.
9. It is possible to grow this plant as a perennial if you can protect it from frost. The plants are usually not as productive as new ones started in spring, but will give you an earlier harvest. Last year I left mine outside and the foliage was killed back by frost, but now that it's warming up a little, to my surprise, a new shoot has emerged. Quite a resilient plant.

PROJECT: GROW SHERBET-FLAVOURED CHILEAN GUAVA BERRIES

In my garden there is an unassuming little shrub in a pot, which in autumn produces the most extraordinary sherbety red berries. Apparently much loved by Queen Victoria, its Latin name is *Ugni molinae* but it also goes by the name of Chilean guava or strawberry myrtle. With little glossy oval evergreen leaves, it produces attractive, beautifully fragrant bell-shaped flowers which are followed by little red berries that I've never seen available to buy in the shops. Although it has survived winter in my garden, it is hardy to about $-5\,°C$ so a hard frost can kill it, and to be safe it's best kept in a sheltered location or greenhouse over winter. I grow mine in a pot, but you can use it to make an edible evergreen hedge in a warm sheltered location, where it can grow to 1.5 metres tall.

When to do it:
You can buy and plant these all year round.

Time from planting to harvest:
You may get a few berries in the first year depending on the size of the plant, and if not, then in the second year.

You will need:
1 Chilean guava plant (the best place to buy this is online)
A large pot
Soil-based potting compost

How to do it:
1. Make sure your pot has good drainage holes and fill the bottom with drainage material such as gravel or broken pieces of pot.
2. Fill the pot with soil-based potting compost and pop your Chilean guava in the centre, at the same depth as it was in the pot.
3. Here there is an option to add mulch (such as gravel or bark chips) to the top of your pot to help retain moisture. This is not a fussy plant, but like anything in a pot it will dry out if you don't water it regularly, and this is especially important when it is in flower.
4. Make sure to enjoy the fragrant blooms when the plant is in flower, as they have a gorgeous scent.
5. This is a late berry to ripen, not ready until mid-autumn. Don't be tempted to pick the fruit as soon as it turns red, as it takes a little longer to reach full sweetness. Make sure to taste one before picking them all – they should be lovely and sweet and packed with flavour.
6. If you want to make more free plants, Chilean guavas can be propagated from cuttings fairly easily, which I do in late summer.

PROJECT: GROW (PINK) BLUEBERRIES

I love growing blueberries – they are perfect for containers, because of their particular need for acidic soil, and in fact I have some plants that are well over a decade old now. You can use these instructions to grow a straightforward blue blueberry, but the variety that produces pink fruits is my personal favourite, as I find them not only especially pretty but also extra sweet. I've never seen pinkberries for sale in the supermarket, which makes them an extra special treat.

When to do it:
Between autumn and early spring.

Time from planting to harvest:
Some blueberry plants may be mature enough to produce fruit in the first year you plant them, but initial harvests can be small. They increase over time as the plants get larger.

You will need:
1 blueberry plant – my personal favourite is pinkberry 'Pink Lemonade', which can be found online
Peat-free acidic compost, known as ericaceous compost
A large container, 30cm for a young plant, moving up to 45cm plus as they get larger
Drainage material
Mulch

How to do it:
1. Give your blueberry plant a good water. Then fill the base of your container with drainage material, such as gravel or broken pots.

2. Blueberry plants don't like drying out, so when choosing your container bear in mind that larger pots dry out more slowly than smaller ones – go for a larger one if you can.
3. Fill the container about halfway up with your ericaceous compost. Now here is a trick to fit your plant perfectly into its hole. Pop your blueberry, complete with its pot, into your container, and check that the height of the top of the soil sits about 2cm below the edge of the container. Fill around the plant, pot and all. Firm down. Now remove your blueberry, take off its pot and drop it back into the perfect hole that's left behind. If your blueberry is rootbound (the roots are tightly coiled around the pot), loosen them with your fingers before putting the plant into the hole.
4. Add a layer of mulch to the top of your container to help retain moisture – I use bark chips or gravel.
5. Water well. Blueberries prefer rainwater, but I rarely have access to that, so tap water will do.
6. Put your blueberry plant in a sunny spot, although they can tolerate a little shade. Keep it well watered, especially when it's flowering and fruiting. Like many fruits, if they dry out during flowering you will end up with a lot less fruit later in the year. Consider putting a plant saucer under your pot to better hydrate it when watering.
7. The plant will benefit from a monthly feed during the growing season – use one formulated for ericaceous (acid-loving) plants.
8. When the berries start to ripen it is worth netting your plants, otherwise you might find the birds get there first.

9. The fruits are ready when they are evenly blue (or pink) all over. They will ripen a few at a time, which means regular small harvests, perfect for snacking or adding to your breakfast of choice. If I get quite a few at once I make blueberry pancakes and compote. Delish.
10. Blueberries don't need to be pruned for the first few years, except to remove any dead wood or crossing branches, but once they are 3–4 years old it is best to remove a third of the oldest branches at the soil level every year to promote new growth. This should be done when the plants are dormant, in late winter.
11. Blueberries can give you fruit for twenty years, and the harvest will increase considerably over the first few years – like many fruits, planting two blueberries of different varieties will improve pollination. It's a good idea to pot up or at least replace some of the soil in the pot every couple of years.

PROJECT: GROW A PATIO APPLE OR PEAR IN A POT

You don't need an orchard to grow abundant fruit trees. Recently I've added a nectarine and a lemon to my ever-expanding collection, but it all started with two fruit trees that have now thrived for many years – my apple and pear. In a good year I've harvested 20–30 fruits from each potted tree. Not only are the fruits a very visually pleasing addition to the garden (baby pears are extremely cute), but these plants are almost worth growing just for the beautiful bee-attracting blossom they burst into every spring.

Fruit trees are a long game, taking a few years to really get going, but it's never too soon to start growing a fruit tree because in a few years' time you'll be so glad you started. I can hardly believe I've had my pear tree for twelve years now, but every year I'm so grateful it's there.

Choosing your tree

Apples and pears are produced by a method called grafting (see page 35). This means that the same variety of fruit, for example a Granny Smith apple, or a Williams pear, can come in various different final sizes of tree, from dwarf, to semi-dwarf, up to vigorous. You want to make sure you choose a plant described as 'dwarf' or 'patio' for container growing.

You can buy trees either in pots or bare-rooted. Bare-root trees are better value and come in a wide range of varieties, but must be planted in winter

when the trees are dormant. Potted fruit trees can be planted any time of year, but spring is ideal. I usually buy my fruit trees online, as this gives you the best range of options.

Many fruit trees need to be pollinated by another tree of the same fruit type but a different variety, so two different kinds of apples that flower at the same time can pollinate each other. I haven't ever had room for more than one apple or pear, and have always found my trees get sufficiently pollinated. That may suggest that there are plenty of fruit trees in London, although when I asked my followers online many of them also had single fruit trees that fruited well. Some varieties are self-fertile and don't need to be pollinated by another tree, so it's worth choosing one of these if you want to be sure of getting fruit.

When to do it:
Bare-root trees must be planted when dormant, between autumn and early spring.
Potted trees can be planted all year round.

How long to harvest:
This can vary depending on the tree – dwarf/patio trees tend to start producing fruit sooner than larger trees but still need a couple of years to get going.

What you'll need:
1 patio apple or pear tree
A deep pot 45cm or more wide
Drainage material
Peat-free soil-based potting mix, such as John Innes No. 3

How to do it:
1. If you are using a bare-root tree, soak the roots in a bucket of water for an hour before planting. If using a potted plant, give it a good water.
2. Choose a nice sunny sheltered spot out of strong winds for your fruit tree – against a south-facing wall is ideal. Pears especially appreciate a warm sheltered spot.
3. Cover the holes in the base of your pot with drainage material such as broken pots or pebbles.
4. Fill the pot halfway up with your potting mix. You want to plant the tree at the same depth it was previously growing, which means either the same depth as in the previous pot or, if using a bare root, it should be possible to see a tidemark on the stem indicating where the plant was previously planted to. Make sure not to bury the graft (you should be able to see a lump on the stem where two trees have been joined) – this needs to sit above the soil.
5. Fill around the tree with the rest of the potting mix, leaving a couple of centimetres gap between the top of the soil and the edge of the pot so that there is room to water easily, and firm the soil in. Top with mulch such as bark or gravel to retain moisture. Water in well.
6. If your pot is deep enough, adding a stake and tying the tree to it can help with stability.
7. In the spring your trees will start to blossom. If any small fruits develop in the first year it is best to remove them – this is so that the plant can use the energy to establish and grow strong instead, giving you better harvests in future years.

8. In the second year you can let a couple of fruits develop if the plant is strong, but if lots of them form, remove the majority.
9. It's a good idea to repot your fruit tree every couple of years and in the process replace some of the soil with fresh compost. Feed your plants every couple of weeks throughout the growing season with a high-potassium feed (such as one formulated for tomatoes).
10. The exact pruning and ongoing care requirements for your tree will depend on what fruit you are growing and the shape the tree is pruned in. For example, I got my apple as a fan-trained tree whereas the pear is a classic goblet shape. Pear and apple trees are pruned in winter, while stone fruits are pruned in spring and summer.

PROJECT: GROW A FIG TREE

Figs are one of my favourite fruits. There are many things I admire about these plants, not least their ability to self-seed in some very hostile environments – I've seen many a fig erupting from a brick wall in the warm climes of the Mediterranean, where they grow like weeds. While it is true that these plants do especially well in places hotter than my London garden, I've also had delicious London figs, and my allotment neighbour has a particularly fine tree. Fig leaves can also be used in cooking – the best ice cream I've ever had was one infused with their flavour. Apparently, you can even use them to make tea.

These plants are also very easy to propagate from cuttings, meaning plenty of free trees if you have the patience and inclination. There is a front garden in south London which is home to a fig tree that I myself grew from a cutting before I moved out years ago. I recently found myself back on my old street, only to find that the fig tree is now huge and laden with fruit just where I left it, planted in a bucket buried in the ground – I was left wistfully wishing I'd dug it up and taken it with me when I moved out!

When to do it:
Spring is the ideal time to plant figs, but potted plants are often available all year round.

Time from planting to harvest:
With all fruit trees there is usually a wait of a year or more before you start to get fruit.

You will need:

A fig tree (choose a variety best suited to your climate – for the UK this is Brown Turkey)

A container 30cm wide (over time the plant may need to be moved to a larger container)

Drainage material, e.g. broken pots, brick or gravel

Peat-free soil-based compost mix, such as John Innes No. 3

How to do it:

1. Start by putting some broken pots, brick or gravel at the bottom of your pot to stop your soil filling up the drainage hole. Fill your container with enough compost so that when you place your fig in the middle it sits a couple of centimetres below the edge of your new container. Remove your fig from its pot and gently tease out any tightly bound roots. Place the rootball in the middle of the new container and fill around it with your compost mix.
2. Leave a gap of a couple of centimetres at the top, so that when you water, the water doesn't just run straight off but sits inside the top of the pot. Firm your fig in and find it a sunny warm spot in your garden – the ideal location is a warm sheltered south-facing wall.
3. Figs can be trained into a fan shape against a sunny wall, which will give you the best fruit yield. This isn't something I have had the space to do in my garden, so I leave mine as a bush.
4. In the spring when fruit appears, start feeding your plants with a high-potassium feed (such as one formulated for tomatoes) every couple of weeks.

5. Figs will usually produce fruitlets (little green figs) a couple of times a year, but only one fruiting tends to ripen in the UK climate. The fruit will be ready to harvest in late summer, when slightly soft to the touch, and should be filled with a rich jammy centre. Depending on the variety, they also change colour from green to purple. I just scoff them off the tree. I couldn't tell you how I'd use them in the kitchen because they never make it that far.
6. In autumn your tree will have unripe figs of various sizes. Remove any larger than a cherry, as these will not survive the winter, leaving just the little embryonic figs behind to ripen next year.
7. It is wise to protect your little embryonic figs from frost over the winter, by wrapping the tree in fleece and/or popping it into a shed.
8. Figs have a tendency to grow long leggy branches, so it's worth cutting back new growth after five leaves in mid-summer. In the winter you can cut any thin or crossing branches completely back to the base, but don't cut the tips of branches as you'll lose your baby figs.

PROJECT: GROW LEMONS

Citrus is a tricky but rewarding challenge, especially if like me you don't have a conservatory or heated greenhouse to keep them in over the winter. However, I think it's well worth the trouble for their beautiful scented blossoms and the excitement of picking your own citrus. I currently have a lemon and a calamansi, but citrus is definitely a collection I plan on expanding. Lemons are the best place to start for a beginner and the most widely available. They will need to be grown in a pot so you can move them during winter.

When to do it:
All year round, but best bought in spring so you can have a summer of growth before the more difficult winter care.

Time from planting to harvest:
You can often buy a lemon tree already flowering or even with fruit on, so it is just a matter of keeping it alive and waiting for that fruit to ripen in winter.

You will need:
1 potted lemon tree
A plant saucer
Summer and winter citrus feed

How to do it:
1. Like other fruit trees, there is little point trying to grow citrus from seed. It will take many years and has no promise of producing good fruit. When buying your lemon tree, choose one that

has flowers or fruit – this way you know it's mature enough to give you a harvest.
2. Pop your new plant into a sunny sheltered spot in your garden. Lemons don't need large pots and are usually sold in pots big enough to last for a couple of years before repotting.
3. Despite being hot-climate plants, lemons hate drying out and can quickly drop leaves if underwatered. Equally they don't want their roots sitting in the damp. So pop your pot in a dish, and make sure to water well regularly, pouring away any water left in the dish after an hour.
4. Lemons are self-fertile and will produce flowers in flushes throughout the year, meaning you can have lemons and flowers on your tree at the same time.
5. To help promote flowering and to prevent leaves from dropping or discolouring, feed your plants once a month with a specially formulated citrus feed. Citrus feeds come in summer and winter formulations, so swap over as you get into late autumn. But don't worry if your plant drops baby fruit – this is very common, as they produce many flowers and so some fruit falls naturally. If slightly larger green fruits suddenly all drop, it means the plant is stressed. When I first got my lemon tree it got too dry, which caused it to drop its baby fruit. When I brought it inside for winter, it again dropped all its baby fruit in response to the sudden change in temperature. It is the first sign the plant is stressed, but it can often easily recover.

6. While citrus will be happy outside in a sunny spot in the summer, it does not like the cold, and while there are occasionally claims about citrus that can survive a light frost, if you want to guarantee your plant won't die it needs protection over the winter. This is where things get a little tricky. A cold greenhouse will not offer enough protection during a prolonged hard frost, and if you bring your citrus inside it won't appreciate being left anywhere dark, draughty or near central heating. I put mine in my living room by a big south-facing window, away from the radiator. But a conservatory is really the perfect place to keep a lemon tree over winter, so if you have one it's basically obligatory in my opinion for you to grow citrus, lest you waste such a perfect opportunity.
7. The fruits ripen slowly, taking 8–12 months, and are ready once they reach full size and turn a rich yellow. You can leave them on the plant until you want to pick them.
8. When moving your citrus back outside in spring, acclimatize it gradually over several days. Once back in the open air it should really cheer up – by late spring mine was flush with new leaves which were quickly followed by an abundance of flowers.
9. When you can see roots appearing through the base of the pot it's time to repot it, which should be done in spring, using a specialist citrus compost. Use a pot only slightly larger than the previous one, as transferring it to a much larger pot will do more harm than good.

10. In the absence of perfect conditions, citrus presents a challenge, but that's sort of what I love about it. And picking my first ever lemons was definitely worth it. If I haven't put you off, give it a go.

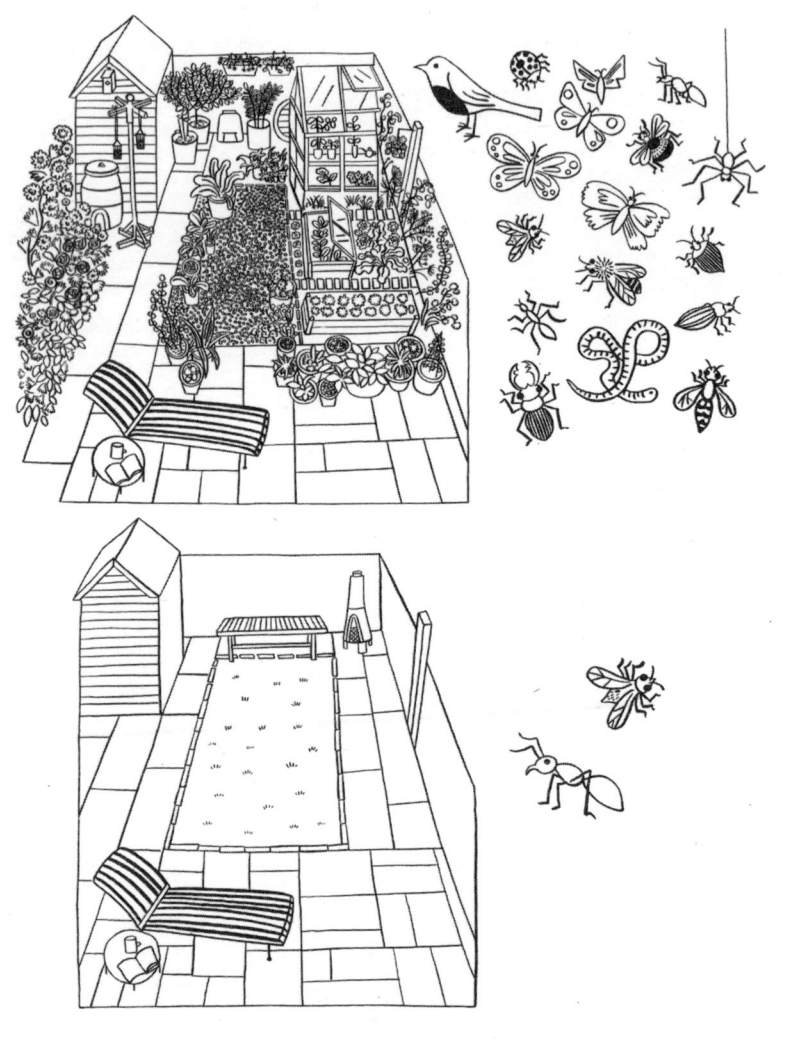

6

HOW TO NURTURE WILDLIFE

This top illustration sums up what I want a garden to be – something that is alive, full of things to explore and creatures to find. For me, extremely neat and manicured gardens lack life. They are a pretence at being around nature, a sort of sanitized outdoor living-room. There is a delicate balance between order and disorder to be struck – I want to have a nice place to sit, I want my veg plants to thrive without too much nibbling, but there is room for nature alongside that.

A pile of logs in a shady corner, slowly rotting down and feeding woodlice and beetle larvae and in turn blackbirds and wrens, frogs and even hedgehogs. A little pond for frogs to spawn in, for dragonfly larvae to hunt prey and hatch and for birds to drink from. Flowers that look pretty but also feed hungry bees, moths and butterflies. Nooks and crannies for creatures to burrow away, eat, sleep, reproduce and hibernate. Creating a garden for nature is about making spaces for them to live, eat, breed and rest. You don't have to do it all at once. Every year I want to find more ways to bring a wider variety of nature to my garden. I think of wildlife as an amazing world in miniature, with all sorts of tiny dramas playing out, things to discover and take you by surprise.

Most of all I encourage you to observe nature, because even just noticing it helps you to get more wonder from it and more interest in it. I recently collected some slug eggs from my compost bin and kept them in a little container just to see how they developed. After weeks and weeks it was possible to see tiny baby slugs inside the little spheres and a week or two after that I opened the container to find tiny little slugs. Do I want them in my garden, no. Will I release them far away, yes. Was it cool to watch nature at work, yes.

Your garden or outdoor space might not be very big, but imagine how many gardens there are when you start to add them all together, in a village, or a town, a city, a whole country. For most of us they are the only piece of 'land' we directly control and the only place we can personally build habitats for nature. You can make a big difference in a small space, and lots of people making a difference in their own gardens adds up.

Why make your garden a space for nature? It's well known that nature is in decline globally, in large part due to habitat loss. In the last twenty years alone, the numbers of flying insects in the UK have dropped by 60%. The UK is now one of the most nature-depleted places on earth. Biodiversity is about how many different species we have – birds, bees, plants, fungi, micro-organisms – all of which are part of the complex ecosystem that we rely on for the air we breathe and the food we eat. But I don't think those kinds of stats often move people to act; they seem somehow far away and bleak, leading maybe to a feeling of helplessness more than a motivation to take action.

Beyond the gloomy outlook is an instinctive and fundamental reason to garden for nature, one that is maybe easier to connect with, not out of fear and guilt but out of joy. Nature has value in and of itself and has the power to soothe and restore, to create wonder and to bring delight. I feed the birds

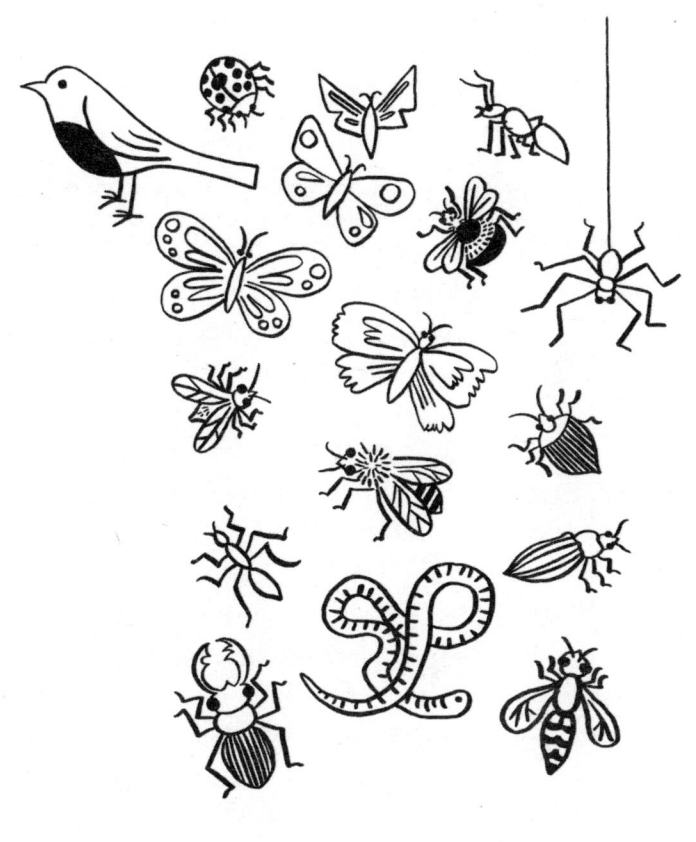

in my garden, yes, because songbird populations have crashed in the last fifty years, but primarily because watching a cute little fluffy blue tit hop on to a feeder and then into a bush to eat a sunflower seed is a thing that draws me out of the everyday. It feels hopeful and exciting every time. If each individual person is motivated by a desire to see and nurture and engage with nature in their own space, imagine that all added up. Your little garden can make a difference to nature and in the process a difference to you.

HOW TO ATTRACT POLLINATORS

Pollinators come in all shapes and sizes – bees, butterflies, lacewings, hoverflies and moths can all be attracted to your garden to find food, namely the sweet nectar in the flowers. Here are a few top tips to help them get what they need.

Plant a variety of pollinator-friendly flowers

To be sure you're catering to a wide variety of insects, fill your garden with a range of different flowers that bloom at different times. When compiling this list I called up the best plantsman I know, my mum, to have a chat. In her garden, where once was lawn is now one huge flower bed which blooms all season and buzzes with life. Whenever I visit we wander round talking about plants and I usually persuade her to dig a chunk up here or there for me to take home. These are the easy-to-grow flowers that fill her (and now my) garden and are alive with pollinators all season long.

Alliums: Ornamental members of the onion family. Planted as bulbs in autumn, they come out in beautiful, often purple, pom-poms in early summer. Bees love them.

Borage: So easy to grow that if you plant it once you'll find it popping up in your garden for ever. It has pretty blue flowers, big furry leaves, and is absolutely loved by bees. The whole plant is also edible (see page 273).

Crocus: A true sign of spring, coming in a range of colours and planted at the same time as grape hyacinths (see below) in autumn. The two together in a hanging basket or container are a very charming combination, alive with bees.

Foxgloves: I think these are one of the most stunning late spring/early summer flowers, and they can be grown from seed, in which case they usually need to be sown the previous year. They're widely available in garden centres in spring, and I usually buy a few and pop them around the garden. Happy in shade, loved by bumblebees.

Grape hyacinths: An early spring flower, clusters of little blue or white florets on a single stem. Planted as bulbs in autumn, they come back year after year.

Honeysuckle: My fence is dripping with it – beautifully scented, grows like a weed, and is loved by long-tongued bumbles and moths.

Lavender: Perhaps the ultimate bee-attracting plant, you can hear lavender literally buzzing with bees when in flower. Different varieties flower at different times, so plant several kinds if you have space to extend the season. It loves a well-drained, sunny spot.

Perennial wallflowers: With many to choose from, a great classic is 'Bowles's Mauve', which produces loads of purple flower stems above grey-green foliage. It's super-easy to grow and flowers for months.

Primroses: Great for a wildlife area or a slightly shady part of your garden, these little yellow wildflowers put on a charming early display and can be divided up and spread around the garden to create new plants.

Red campion: A woodland wildflower with jolly, bright pink blooms, red campion is happy in shadier parts of the garden and is loved by bees, hoverflies and butterflies.

***Salvia* 'Hot Lips':** The sage family (*Salvia*) includes lots of pollinator-friendly plants. I have three different kinds of salvia in my garden and I'd say my mum has many more. 'Hot Lips' is a widely available variety with a memorable name, which when it comes to plants always helps. A perennial, it is super-easy to grow and flowers for months with the little white and red flowers that give it its name. Loved by all sorts of pollinators.

Valerian: A perennial flower that produces an abundance of little white or pale pink flower clusters. It has a heady scent and its roots are commonly used in herbal sleeping medicines. It can be grown from seed, cuttings or by dividing established clumps. It attracts just about everything, from bees and butterflies to flies and beetles.

Don't use pesticides

Many pesticides are extremely toxic to bees and other pollinators. Chemical pesticides are one of the main causes for the decline in insects, birds and other forms of wildlife that we've seen in recent times. They will often kill more than the intended target or harm creatures that feed on the bug you are trying to kill. For example, aphids are food for ladybirds, lacewing larvae, hoverflies, house martins, swallows, wrens and more, so spray them with poison and plenty of other creatures won't thank you for it. Gardens that are allowed to thrive with a wide variety of life are often more resilient, and the various insects, pests and their predators come to even each other out. So if you want a living garden full of beneficial insects to pollinate your plants, leave the pesticides in the garden centre, let a few bugs munch here and there and check out page 49 for how to deal with pests in a low-impact, organic way.

Let your lawn flower

Since 1930, 97% of the UK wildflower meadows have disappeared and along with them all the food and habitats they provided for nature. So why not try out 'No-Mow May' and leave your grass uncut for the month, when many wildflower species are in bloom. This simple action can significantly increase the nectar available to hungry pollinators, and leaving your lawn long at different times of the year will benefit different wildflowers and insects. So when you can, leave your grass long. At the end of each 'No-Mow May', count the number of different species that have popped up and take note.

PROJECT: MAKE A BEE DRINKING STATION

This is a very easy way to help bees in your garden. Like all living things, bees need water; however, they need it not only to drink for themselves but to carry back to their nests for their young. They can be at risk of drowning in deep bodies of water, so making a bee drinking station is the perfect bee-friendly solution.

When to do it:
All year round, but especially in the warmer months.

You will need:
A shallow dish
A plant pot to stand it on (optional)
Some pebbles

How to do it:
1. Arrange a selection of different sized pebbles and stones in the dish (you can also use clay balls, twigs or moss). You want to create different levels for bees to land on so they can take a few sips without getting wet.
2. Add water to your dish, making sure that there are plenty of surfaces above the water for the bees to land on.
3. You can raise it off the ground by popping it on top of an upturned pot.
4. Put the dish on its upturned pot among bee-friendly flowers.
5. Replace and top up the water in your dish regularly.

THE POWER OF DEAD WOOD AND OTHER HABITATS

Dead wood and old leaves are not an unsightly mess to be removed from your garden, but instead are a vital part of the natural living ecosystem. They provide habitat and shelter for all sorts of creatures and provide nutrients to the soil.

During growth, plants take in nutrients from the soil, and when they die or drop their leaves the dead matter is then broken down by organisms living in the soil, making it available to plants again. There are loads of organisms, from tiny soil microbes and fungi to beetle larvae and woodlice, that feed off dead plant matter and in the process recycle nutrients in your garden.

In fact, dead wood is so important to various insects that there is a whole group of them known as saproxylic, coming from the Greek words *sapros*, meaning rotten, and *xylon*, meaning wood. Around 650 species of UK beetle require dead wood for at least part of their life cycle. My personal favourite, and one I have loved since I was a child, is the stag beetle, the UK's largest beetle and really a very special thing to spot – their larvae spend up to six years underground, feeding on rotten wood. All this is to say that log piles and dead leaves are great habitats for nature and an easy way to make your garden more wildlife-friendly.

PROJECT: HOW TO BUILD A LOG PILE

Don't collect logs from nature spots to build your log pile, as they may already be being used by wildlife and you will risk destroying existing habitats. A local tree surgeon may be happy to gift you some logs – this is where my dad gets logs for his woodburning stove, and I always steal a few to make little habitats for nature. Alternatively use trimmings from hedges, ask your neighbours, or even buy a bag of logs.

When to do it:
All year round.

You will need:
15 or so logs (don't use treated wood)
Dried leaves and sticks
A spade
2 thick sticks to use as posts

OPTIONAL:

Primroses
Ferns
Wild garlic

How to do it:
1. Pick a spot in shade that will ideally stay damp all year round. Mark out the area for your log pile and drive two upright sticks in at either end to hold your logs in place.
2. If possible, dig a trench between the two sticks the depth of your largest logs so that you can bury the bottom layer. This will attract the largest array of wildlife, as the logs come in contact

with the soil and will start to decompose quicker, providing food for those saproxylic insects.
3. With the cut ends of the logs facing you, starting with your largest logs at the bottom, lay them down side by side in a row between the two upright sticks. Once you have your first layer, fill any gaps with sticks and dried leaves before stacking more logs on top. Repeat with layers of logs, dried leaves and sticks, building your log pile into a pyramid shape.
4. Consider adding a stumpery – to do this you will need long logs that can be buried upright. The benefit of a stumpery is that it provides additional habitats for creatures such as stag beetle larvae that feed on wood specifically buried underground. Dig an individual hole for each log so they aren't touching, and bury them 50cm deep to provide the best habitats for those underground critters. Firm the soil back around the upright logs to hold them in place.
5. To make it an even more attractive feature you can add shade-loving woodland plants such as primroses and ferns, and also wild garlic, which will create shelter and habitats for more wildlife.
6. Water your log pile and keep it moist to make it the best habitat for a wide range of creatures.

THE JOY OF BIRDS

One of the things I love to do most in my garden is watch the birds. It also reminds me that nature really does appear when you invite it in. When I look out of my window my garden often has birds in it, not just blue tits, great tits, sparrows and the occasional robin on the feeders, but also dunnocks twitching around on the ground beneath, wrens in the honeysuckle, a blackbird in the veg patch. And after a year and a half of waiting I finally saw a pair of beautiful goldfinches this week.

It can take time and patience to attract birds to your garden. At first I went a little overboard, with multiple feeders full of all kinds of different things, from peanuts and sunflower seeds to suet balls and pellets. I put out fruit, bread, mealworms, even dried insects, in an attempt to attract as many birds as quickly as possible. In the end I had to wait weeks, if not months, for the birds to discover the excessive feast I had put on. Every day I would peer out of the window hoping to spot something.

The first visitor to my bird feeding station was a neighbour's cat, which having smelled the insect and crustacean mix climbed all the way up to the top of the feeding tree and sat on top of it. The next visitor was a squirrel. Then a magpie. One day I spotted a wren, which as it happens had nothing to do with my feeders, given that they scurry around catching small insects. Then finally a little blue tit arrived on the feeder and I was so delighted. Incidentally, the lesson of the wren is an important one – feeders are great for attracting birds but so is planting plenty of cover for them to perch and hide in and feed themselves berries and insects.

Turning your space into a haven for our feathered friends will bring an ever-changing landscape of birds going through the rhythm of their lives. Recently sparrows and great tits brought their newly fledged young to my garden, where they sat like little fluffy balls among the foliage, squawking to be fed by attentive parents. Tell me the thought of that doesn't warm your heart.

How to attract birds

While putting up a bird-feeder is great way to attract birds to your garden, do consider some bird-friendly planting to give them both food and protection when they come to visit.

Plants for birds

There are several ways that plants can provide food for birds, the most obvious being berries and seeds, but plants that attract insects and provide cover also attract insectivorous birds like little wrens. Having plenty of cover near your bird-feeder also allows the birds to grab a morsel of food and retreat to the safety of the foliage to eat it before coming back. For plants to grow up fences, check out page 285. Here are a few fantastic plants that have benefits to a whole host of wildlife but will be especially good at providing food and shelter to visiting birds.

Cotoneaster: These shrubs are a great source of nectar for pollinating insects when their pink and white flowers arrive in early summer – they are laden with red berries in autumn, loved by a whole host of garden birds. There are lots of different cultivars to choose from, to suit even the smallest spaces.

Dandelions: These get a bad rap as a quickly spreading deep-rooted weed, but dandelions are actually fantastic wildflowers, providing plenty of forage for bees. They have many culinary and medicinal uses, but also are a favoured food of goldfinches, which many a time I've watched hopping about grassy areas pulling out the fluffy seeds.

Ivy: Thickly covering fences or walls, ivy creates a huge array of habitats for wildlife and of feeding and nesting spots for birds. Attracting insects that attract insectivorous birds, it also provides much-loved berries in winter.

Sunflowers: There is nothing jollier than a sunflower in bloom, especially when you find bees sleeping in them. But leave the flower heads on until the seeds are mature, or cut them and hang them in your garden for the birds to pull out the seeds. The sunflowers in my garden last year actually self-seeded after falling out of the bird-feeder. I left them to grow and they were a lovely addition to the wildlife area.

Teasel: These tall, spiky, architectural biennial plants have striking seed heads that stand throughout the winter and add interest in the colder months. They easily self-seed and can often be found growing wild, in grassland, wastelands and car parks. The seed heads are loved by birds such as goldfinches.

PROJECT: PUT OUT A BIRD-FEEDER

Feeding the birds is especially important in the months when food is scarce and the weather is cold. On very cold days you may notice extra visits from hungry birds, so make sure to keep feeders topped up so birds aren't using their precious energy to visit an empty feeder. There are lots of different bird foods available, designed to attract a range of different birds, so try out a few different ones to see what is popular with your local birds.

When to do it:
All year round.

You will need:
A bird-feeder or two
Bird food
A place to put your feeders, out of reach of predators
Patience!

How to do it:
1. **Choose your bird-feeder:** There are loads of options when it comes to bird-feeders. To attract the widest variety of birds it's worth having a couple of different hanging feeders, or you could try a bird-table if you have room, which you can put a variety of foods on. Bear in mind that birds have different feeding habits and so will prefer different kinds of feeders – some birds, such as robins, blackbirds and dunnocks, are natural ground feeders and are most likely to be spotted scooping up dropped seed. A robin will often have an ungainly attempt at eating from a

hanging feeder, but will prefer a bird-table or tray they can stand on. Tits on the other hand can easily eat from a feeder with no perch, holding on to the mesh with their little feet. Here are a few common types:

- **Metal cages and tubes with large holes:** For suet balls and blocks.
- **Tubes with medium mesh:** For peanuts.
- **Tubes made of fine mesh or plastic:** For small seeds like niger and sunflower.
- **A covered table:** This can accommodate a range of foods, including fruit and mealworms as well as seeds.
- **A hanging covered bowl:** There are lots of ornamental bird-feeders you can hang around your garden – the cover keeps the food dry and birds can happily perch on the edge.
- **Window feeders:** You can get clear feeders that attach to your window. They have mixed success, but if birds do visit you get a great view!
- **Squirrel-proof feeders:** Squirrels love bird food and they will rapidly munch through piles of it, so it's worth considering a squirrel-proof feeder. There are various kinds – some that have a bird-feeder inside a cage, and others where a tube slides down if anything too heavy climbs on! They can be expensive but are worth the investment if you have a lot of hungry squirrels.
- **Ground feeders:** You can put feed out for ground-feeding birds in a dish or sprinkle a little on the ground, but make sure it's in an open area

where they can easily spot any predators. I find ground-feeding birds are happy to scoop any seed that falls from the feeders above.

2. **Choose your feed:** Different feeds attract different birds, and different feeders are also designed to hold different foods. This all makes it sound rather complicated, but ultimately, it's good to try out a few feeds, see what your local birds like and go with that.

- **Sunflower seeds:** A hugely popular all-round crowd pleaser. To attract the widest range of birds, go for sunflower seeds that have been removed from the shells. Robins, tits, finches, sparrows, dunnocks, blackbirds and even woodpeckers will be happy to munch on them, to name just a few.
- **Peanuts:** Peanuts are a great winter food source for tits. Always put them in a feeder so small pieces can be nibbled off – and they should be avoided in spring, as they could choke chicks if a parent tried to use them to feed their young.
- **Mealworms:** Especially loved by blackbirds and robins.
- **Niger seeds:** These are popular with finches, so may help attract them to your garden if they are present in the area. They often need a special feeder, as the seeds are very small.
- **Seed mixes:** Cheaper seed mixes are often bulked out with cereals like wheat, oats and corn that many birds aren't a huge fan of.
- **Suet balls, blocks and logs:** These are fat blocks mixed with things like seeds and insects

which birds nibble bits off – I find them to be hugely popular in my garden. They attract a wide range of birds such as tits, robins, sparrows, blackbirds. But they also often attract the attention of squirrels and pigeons. They are a great high-energy source of food in winter, but don't let them sit too long in your feeders in summer as the fat can go rancid.

3. **Position your bird-feeder:** Put your feeder high enough up off the ground that it is out of reach of cats. You can hang feeders from trees, from a bird-feeding station, or as I do, from the arch in the middle of the garden. I find that the birds like having things to hop on and off nearby, like the bars on the arch and the branches of a potted shrub. I've hung up a branch of rosehips next to the feeder, which birds like robins like to stand on to peck the suet logs. Don't put it too near any dense bushes that a predator could surprise your birds from.

4. **Be patient:** It can take weeks or more for birds to find your feeder, so don't be disheartened if they don't arrive straight away. Do try positioning feeders in different places to see what is most popular with your feathered friends.

5. **Keep your feeders stocked up and clean:** Don't leave food sitting in the feeders for weeks uneaten, and especially don't let it get mouldy, but do top up your feeders regularly when they are nearly empty. Birds come to rely on known sources of food. Keep your feeders clean to prevent spreading diseases.

6. **Enjoy the birds:** When they do arrive, take time to remember or take a note of what birds you see, and observe what they are up to. I recently saw sparrows eating aphids off my rosebuds before popping to the feeder for a little snack. Sparrows are a new addition to my garden after a year of having the feeders out. A joy to see.

PROJECT: HOW TO BUILD A MINI WILDLIFE POND

Without a doubt the garden project that has brought me the most joy has been building a wildlife pond. One of my dearest friends, who I've known since primary school, loves frogs, and so one cold winter's day in February she came to keep me company while I set about making our joint amphibian dreams a reality. Three years later I can declare the pond, which measures just 60cm square, a huge success: the frogs arrived after a year, laid eggs in the second year, and I now have a pond teeming with tiny frogs, damselfly larvae and water snails. I could watch it for hours. A whole miniature world brought to life by the wildlife that decided to make it their home.

You can make a pond in the smallest of spaces, and as long as you get the right aquatic plants there's no need for a pump or filter. People sometimes ask where the wildlife comes from, or whether I put any of the creatures in there. The answer is no. Frogs can travel up to 500 metres from their breeding pond, toads up to a kilometre and the tiny palmate newt up to 19 kilometres: build it and they will come!

When to do it:
Any time, but autumn or late winter will allow your pond to settle in best.

Time from building to wildlife spotting:
Though your pond will start providing habitats for nature from the first day (often birds are the first to arrive, for a drink and a bath!), it can take time to

attract a wide variety of wildlife. Every pond is different, and all will provide useful habitats.

You will need:
A large watertight container – a preformed pond, an old sink or a wooden barrel
Builders' sand
Gravel
Stones/pebbles
Slate/bricks to build ledges
Aquatic plants – more information below

How to do it:
1. **First pick a suitable container to make your pond:** This doesn't need to be complicated: you can use a large washing-up bowl, a preformed pond liner, or an upcycled old barrel or sink, making sure to fill any holes. My little pond is 70 litres, made from a 60cm square container designed as a water feature reservoir. Alternatively you can use a pond liner and fleece underlay to line a hole you've dug to your desired shape and depth. You can even create your pond in a container on a patio, but for the best access for wildlife, sink it into the ground.

2. **Pick your location:** The ideal spot for your pond will have some sun, but avoid a spot that bakes in the sun all day. If you can, choose a spot with a little space around it to create a mini wildlife area. If you are sinking your pond into the ground, dig a hole big enough to pop your container into. Remove any sharp stones and, if using a soft liner, cover the base of the hole with builders' sand.

3. **Pop your container into the hole and make sure it's nice and snug**: Surround your pond with further habitats for nature by planting low-lying pollinator-friendly plants and adding bricks, logs and old broken terracotta pots. Hide the edges of your pond with large pebbles or stones. A slate or two overhanging the edge will create a shady spot in your pond that will be popular with frogs.

4. **Start filling the inside of your pond:** Aim to create plenty of nooks and crannies for different creatures to live in.
   - First cover the base of your pond with a layer of sand and gravel, then add some larger stones.
   - Next, create different levels, using bricks, stones and pieces of slate so that you have shallower ledges that will sit just 5–10cm below the surface of the water. This not only provides more varied habitats but is also the perfect place to put your marginal pond plants.
   - Adding pebbles or small logs to these ledges will give birds and insects places to perch, drink and wash in the shallow parts of the pond.
   - It's also good to include a little ramp, such as a plank of wood weighted down in the water with a brick at one end, so that there is an exit route for any non-water-loving wildlife that might fall in.

5. **Fill up your pond with rainwater:** If you can, use rainwater, but if that's not possible you can make do with tap water. If using tap water, it's

best to leave your pond for a couple of weeks before adding your plants.

6. **Next add your plants:** To keep things simple when I'm making a little wildlife pond, I've found a British native wildlife planting scheme from a reputable online supplier which includes all the different kinds of plant and mini pond needs. It's best not to use plants from existing ponds, as this can spread disease. Pond plants are best planted in aquatic baskets and aquatic soil.

   - Include one or two submerged plants that sit below the surface of the water and that provide cover and oxygen. Sometimes known as oxygenators, this includes plants like hornwort, water starwort and spiked water milfoil.
   - Plant several marginals in the shallows, such as water forget-me-not, marsh marigold, brooklime, lesser spearwort and corkscrew rush.
   - Include a submerged plant with floating leaves to provide shelter for tadpoles and dragonfly larvae, as well as a place for water snails and newts to lay their eggs, such as a small water lily, or frogbit.

7. **Let it settle in:** Once your pond is built, it can take several months to get into balance. Initially nothing much may happen for a few weeks, except maybe a few mosquito larvae. The water can be quite murky and green, and it might get slimy bubbles on the surface. Then after a few months a close look at the water will find it absolutely teeming with tiny creatures. Blood

worms build little mud nests all over the walls and later hatch out into non-biting midges, and water fleas and tiny beetles busily teem around. It's quite amazing to watch. These of course will later form the basis of an important food chain in your pond, so their arrival is definitely a sign that things are going in the right direction. Over time the plants start to filter and clean the water and it naturally changes, becoming much clearer. This was the point when my frogs arrived and they've been there ever since, often sitting in the shallows under an overhanging slate, or having a sunbath on the wildlife ladder.

8. **Minimal maintenance:** There is very little work involved in keeping your pond happy and it is best left undisturbed. It is OK for your pond level to drop in warm weather, but if it is at risk of drying out, top it up using rainwater. If you have to use tap water, leave it for a couple of days in a bucket to allow chlorine to evaporate before adding it to your pond. Too much shade can reduce oxygen in the water, so make sure to cut back any surrounding plants that become too tall. Do this by hand, to avoid harming any creatures that may be living in the plants. Remove excess leaves in autumn, as too much organic matter can make the water go stagnant.

9. **Enjoy your pond:** Take time to look and see what new creatures have arrived. They may be extremely small, but all are fascinating. If you don't know what something is, do a little

research – it's very satisfying when you can put a name to the critters you find in your pond. I was amazed to find tiny clams recently, and have since found out they are called European fingernail clams!

7

HOW TO GROW FLOWERS

It took me a while to appreciate flowers, blindsided as a new gardener by the excitement and possibilities of growing veg. These days I am obsessed with finding and adding new blooms for every season to my already very full garden.

I aim to have a stream of little cut-flower bouquets around the flat from early spring until late autumn. If that means just a single stemmed daffodil sometimes, then so be it. I've filled my home with little vases perfect for celebrating even the most modest of stems. I especially love flowers with gorgeous scents, so that even indoors you can smell the garden. As I write this, I am sitting next to a collection of different white and yellow scented narcissus, a pink hyacinth, two different tulips and a few little stems of blue muscari. These days I can't get enough of them, and I could just stare at them for hours.

Here I have included some of the first and easiest flowers I grew in my garden – jolly spring bulbs, sweet peas, summer cut flowers and of course a few edible ones too. For some pollinator-friendly flowers, check out page 232, and those good for attracting birds can be found on page 243.

SPRING BULBS

Spring flowers are one of the most anticipated arrivals in my garden each year. You will find bulbs widely available in garden centres and even in large supermarkets in autumn, which is when they need to be planted in order to flower in spring. Many are extremely easy to grow and look great in pots or planted directly in the ground. I like to get both a range of different flowers and different varieties of the same flower (which will flower at different times), so planting a selection will give you blooms from late winter to early summer.

Alliums: Alliums are true stunners of the late spring and early summer garden, arriving just as the tulips and other spring flowers are coming to an end. Planted during autumn, these ornamental onions like plenty of water to reach their full potential. I prefer to grow them directly in the ground, where they seem happier than in pots. Pollinators absolutely adore them.

Crocuses: These little spring pops of colour couldn't be easier to grow or more welcome in the bare landscape of late winter. I pop them into pots around other plants, use them as the top layer in a bulb lasagna (page 262) or plant them in the wildlife area. These flowers naturalize over time, so if they are planted in an open site and are happy, they will spread and produce more flowers each year.

Grape hyacinths/muscari: Pretty little clusters of flowers on thin stems that come in blue and white, these are much loved by bees and last a long time. They work really well in arrangements with other flowers such as crocuses, primroses and miniature daffodils. Like crocuses, they self-seed and naturalize easily.

Hyacinths: Hugely popular due to their incredible scent and gorgeous colours, hyacinths have a single thick stem covered with individual fleshy tubular flowers. They prefer free-draining soil and do best in sun. They have a bit of a habit of flopping over, so may need some support when in bloom.

Irises: Bulb irises can produce some of the earliest spring flowers. Dwarf varieties are especially small and cute, and flower very early in the year, while Dutch irises are produced on taller stems and arrive later in the spring and early summer. Very easy to grow and great in pots or in the ground.

Narcissus: More commonly known as daffodils, there are so many different ones to choose from. Super-easy to grow, they are planted in autumn for spring colour. My favourites are small multi-headed varieties like Minnow and beautifully scented ones like Pheasant's Eye.

Tulips: Plant in autumn for spring colour. They come in loads of different varieties and are very easy to grow. Perfect in pots or in borders. Plant them twice the depth of the bulb. They make a fabulous cut flower, or you can just enjoy them in the garden. Some flower early and others much later, meaning that a few different varieties can keep you in tulips for several months.

PROJECT: HOW TO MAKE A BULB LASAGNA

The beauty of a bulb lasagna is that you can plant layers of different bulbs in the same pot and they will flower in waves, giving you a changing display that lasts a couple of months. In fact, the first things I ever planted in my garden were three pots of spring bulbs. On a whim I'd bought a load of daffodil and tulip bulbs, which I then forgot about completely until mid-November. Realizing it was now or never, I set about planting as many as I could in the only three pots I owned. The bulb lasagna method turned out to be the best use of space and they were such a success! First the pots were filled with a whole array of different daffodils, delicate miniature multi-headed ones, loud gaudy frilly ones – all a delight – and just as they finished, waves of striking tulips filled their place. In subsequent years I have added extra layers and tried a combination of different bulbs. They never disappoint. This little project takes literally minutes to get set up and then all you need to do is wait.

When to do it:
Mid-autumn to mid-winter.

Time from planting to bloom:
3–6 months, depending on what you plant and when you plant them.

You will need:
A selection of spring-flowering bulbs – crocus, daffodils and tulips make a great combination,

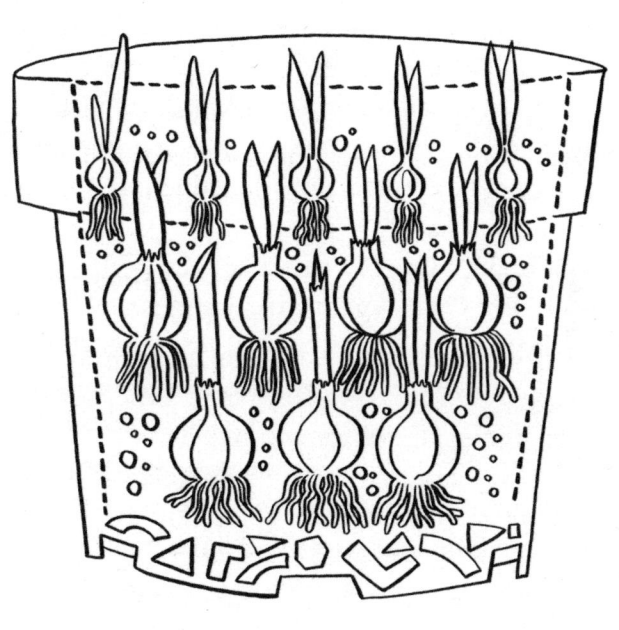

but you can experiment with different spring flowers and arrangements

A 30cm pot, but adjust the number of bulbs for different-sized planters

Peat-free multipurpose compost

How to do it:
1. Add a handful of gravel or some broken terracotta pots to the bottom of your pot to improve drainage. Fill the pot one third full with compost.
2. You can plant the bulbs a lot closer than the suggested spacing on the packet. Start with tulips, spaced approximately 6–8 in a 30cm pot, making sure the bulbs are not touching. Cover with compost.
3. Next make a layer of miniature daffodils, again 6–8 bulbs. Cover again with compost.
4. Finally make a layer of 12–15 crocuses. Make sure your top layer of bulbs is buried at least twice their own depth.
5. Water in, then ideally lift the pots off the ground. I pop mine on some shelving. My mum swears by this, as the best way to stop the bulbs getting too damp and cold as opposed to leaving them on the ground.
6. Your pots will need very little maintenance over the winter. If they get bone dry, give them a bit of water. During the winter months little green shoots will appear.
7. Squirrels can be a problem, as they like nothing more than digging up bulbs. I cover pots with bramble branches or tie a criss-cross of twine over the top of the pot. Chicken wire is also very effective.

8. Your crocuses will be the first to appear in late winter, followed by daffodils and then tulips, which should keep you in flowers until mid- to late spring. Depending on what you plant and the weather, in any one year varieties sometimes arrive at the same time, giving you a stunning display.
9. Once your flowers have finished, don't be tempted to cut off the leaves if you want the bulbs to flower again. Remove the flower heads, feed the plants and let them die back naturally. The bulbs can be lifted and planted again in the autumn, but not all bulbs will flower again for another year. I prefer to remove the plants from the pot when green and plant the whole lot out in a garden border. Then anything that comes up the next year is a nice surprise.

Alternative arrangements:
I have planted many different combinations of spring bulbs in pots and hanging baskets, and here are a few others I particularly enjoyed:

- You can top your spring bulb arrangements with winter-flowering bedding plants such as primroses or pansies. I particularly enjoyed red winter primroses with blue muscari and dwarf narcissus Minnow in pale yellow.

- White muscari make a great alternative to crocuses in an arrangement of daffodils and tulips. Appearing later than crocuses, the little white clusters nestle between the stems of the other flowers. They are for planting in the top layer in place of the crocuses.

- Purple crocuses and blue muscari in a hanging basket put on a beautiful display, especially when they are all in flower together and buzzing with bees. This wasn't strictly a lasagna, I just mixed both bulbs together in a densely planted layer.

PROJECT: HOW TO MAKE A SPRING FLOWERING BED BORDER

This is a great way to use up any spare bulbs you have left after filling pots. It's extremely easy, and something I did when I found some extra bags of bulbs in a cupboard. That's the beauty of spring bulbs, you don't need to do anything fancy to get a gorgeous display. Veg beds can look a little bare in the spring, and I love having a border of successional spring flowers, which also attracts bees. It takes 10 minutes to do and can be enjoyed for months. Different tulips will flower at different times, so planting two or three different varieties will often mean you get new flowers popping up over a longer period.

When to do it:
Mid-autumn to mid-winter.

Time from planting to bloom:
3–6 months, depending on what you plant and when you plant them.

You will need:
A selection of spring bulbs, such as a range of different tulips and narcissus and alliums
A strip 20cm wide along the edge of a bed

How to do it:
1. Dig a trench 15cm deep along the edge of your veg or flower bed, then simply fill it with bulbs. As you open each new bag, spread them along the whole length so that your display will have an even arrangement of different flowers across its length.

2. Avoid the bulbs touching each other, but really pack them in for a succession of colour in spring.
3. Cover over with soil again and water in.
4. Cover the ground over winter with some sticks or bamboo canes to deter digging squirrels.
5. Your bulbs will look after themselves, popping up with different flowers and combinations appearing throughout spring and early summer.

PROJECT: GROW SWEET PEAS FROM SEED

Sweet peas for me are a must in any garden. They aren't edible but they are very productive, by which I mean that I have fresh sweet peas in my house, filling the air with their incredible fragrance, all summer long. From just a handful of plants I harvest a bouquet every few days and have them from June until September. Sweet peas are great planted in the ground or in pots, but they will need something to climb up, such as a tepee of canes or a plant obelisk. I like to combine them with climbing beans on an archway.

When to do it:
Sweet peas can be sown in autumn if you have a greenhouse to keep them in over winter, to give you an earlier display, but I usually sow mine in spring.

Time from planting to bloom:
12–14 weeks.

You will need:
Sweet pea seeds
Pots or module tray
Peat-free multipurpose compost
Something for the sweet peas to climb up – I use an archway, but a tepee of canes (page 25) or even strings up a fence (page 92) would also work
Twine

How to do it:
1. Soak your seeds overnight in water to help them germinate.

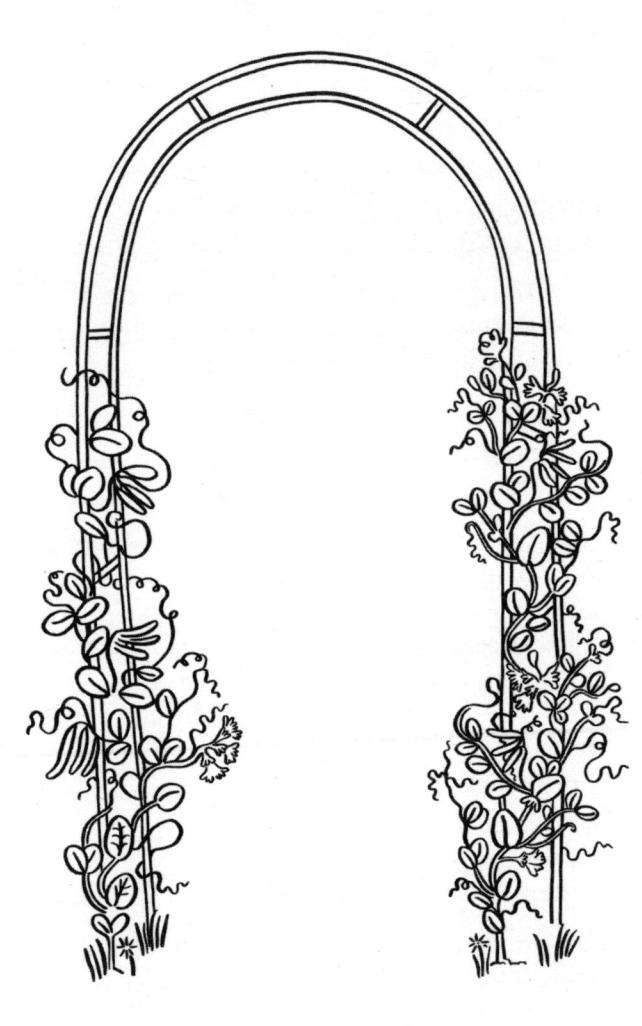

2. Sow the seeds in modules or pots of peat-free multipurpose compost – you can sow a couple of seeds per module or 4–5 seeds in a 12cm pot. Covering your tray with a propagator lid or popping a sandwich bag over your pots will stop them drying out until the seedlings appear.
3. Germinate on a sunny windowsill from late winter, or outside with protection (such as a mini greenhouse) from mid-spring.
4. Once the plants get two sets of leaves, pinch out the tops of the plants. You can just snip them off with scissors. This will encourage the plant to produce side shoots at the point at which each leaf meets the stem. Bushier plants means more flowers in the long run.
5. Sweet peas are hardy annuals, meaning that indoor-raised plants can be moved outside in mid-spring and will tolerate a light frost. However, like all indoor-raised plants they will still need gradual hardening off to avoid shocking the plants (page 32).
6. Prepare the ground with organic matter such as peat-free compost and a little blood, fish and bone. I dig a small trench next to my archway and plant 3–5 plants along its 30cm side. If doing a tepee, I plant a couple of plants at the base of each cane. This is closer than traditional spacing, but I find it gives me an abundance of blooms in a small area.
7. Water them in well, and as the plants grow, tie the stems to the supports. They can climb a little themselves, but tying them in stops them flopping over and going off in unwanted directions.

8. Pick your sweet peas regularly once they start to flower. They make great cut flowers, so fill your house with little bouquets. If you miss any flowers they will rapidly turn into seed pods – remove these to keep the plants producing more blooms.
9. Feed your plants every 1–2 weeks with a liquid feed high in potassium (such as tomato feed) and keep them well watered. With care, sweet peas can flower for 3 months or more.

GROW EDIBLE FLOWERS

Edible flowers are a reminder to be inquisitive about plants and to see them beyond the confines of what the supermarkets offer us. Cucumbers, courgettes, squashes, beans, garlic flower shoots, the unopened buds of capers, flowers on chives, fennel, lavender, roses and tulips are just some of the edible flowers you might find in your garden. Always check and make sure a flower is edible before you try it – just because you can eat part of the plant doesn't mean you can eat all of it. Tomatoes and potatoes, for example, have poisonous flowers and foliage.

If you are new to growing edible flowers and want to easily keep track of the plants you are growing, try potting them up together in a large container – then you'll know exactly where to go when you want flowers to decorate salads, cakes or to pop into a drink. Borage can grow to quite a size, so is best left in the ground, but nasturtiums with their trailing habit work well around the edges of a container, which is gorgeous filled in the middle with camomile and cornflowers.

Below are five of my favourite edible flowers. Some are super-easy to sow direct, such as cornflowers and borage, while nasturtiums and camomile make great container plants.

Borage

Borage is an edible flower that grows like a weed, in fact it's popped up in just about every pot, border and even the gravel in my garden this year. It's loved by pollinators and is entirely edible. Until recently I'd only ever eaten the little star-shaped blue flowers, which taste like cucumber, but it turns out the greens are popular in Italy, Spain and Greece, where they are used to stuff pasta and make soups. I had some beautiful borage greens in Rome, and I am now a convert. This is what I love about edible things – just because one culture doesn't have a tradition of using a plant in a certain way, it doesn't mean somewhere else in the world there isn't a tradition that locals wouldn't think twice about.

How to grow:
Borage is an annual, meaning it lives for one year and needs to be started from seed again each spring. However, once you've grown borage you will often find it pops up of its own accord around the garden, as it easily self-seeds. It's happiest when sown direct where it is to grow, so sprinkle the seeds in a sunny spot, cover lightly and water in. The plants may need staking, as they can reach nearly a metre tall. I often pick the blue flowers and use them in drinks or to decorate food.

Calendula

Like borage, calendula just comes up in my garden. Chuck a few seeds in the direction of some soil and you'll have it forever more. What I love about this flower is how incredibly bright and jolly it is – almost iridescent orange, it shines like a beacon. It has so many uses that it is a lot more than just an edible flower. The edible petals, although a little bitter, can be made into tea, used to decorate cakes, dye clothes, and they have medicinal properties. Calendula is loved by pollinators and I think it's a very charming cut flower too.

How to grow:
In spring or early summer, sprinkle some seeds on to an open, sunny patch of ground. They will be happy in ordinary soil, which can be fairly poor and dry. Cover with a little soil, water in, and they'll soon pop up. Be sure to deadhead finished flowers to keep the plants in bloom.

Cornflower

Happy to be sown direct, these colourful little flowers go by the name of bachelor's buttons in America. While extremely popular as a garden flower, they are one of the lesser-known edible blooms; it is the petals you eat and whilst they aren't hugely flavoursome they are very pretty and can be used fresh or dried and make especially good cake decorations.

How to grow:

Seeds can be sown direct in a little trench where you want them to flower, or you can simply scatter them over the ground and cover them lightly with soil. Like many plants, they prefer well-drained, moist soil in a sunny location. The blooms are fairly short-lived, so make a few sowings to keep them blooming in your garden.

PROJECT: MAKE A NASTURTIUM HANGING BASKET

This plant is so much more than an edible flower. The entire thing is edible, and the baby leaves of the nasturtium are in vogue with top chefs, often adding a final flourish to the most high end of dishes. The flowers are bright and peppery with a hint of sweetness, the mature leaves can be cooked like spinach, and the young seed pods can be pickled. It's easy to grow, in fact in many countries it grows like a weed. The pollinators love it and it often works as a great decoy – or companion plant – for brassicas, attracting cabbage white butterflies, which lay their eggs on it instead of on your prize kale. They grow rapidly, are covered in a multitude of flowers which come in loads of colours, you can get varieties with variegated leaves, and they flower from mid-summer until the first frost. Basically. Grow this plant.

When to do it:
Spring.

Time from planting to flowering:
Approx. 6 weeks.

You will need:
Nasturtium seeds or plants (if you want something compact, choose a dwarf variety)
A hanging basket
Peat-free multipurpose compost
A hanging basket bracket
Grit or perlite (optional)

How to do it:
1. You can start your seeds in modules or small pots but they are easy to sow direct.
2. Make sure your hanging basket has drainage holes and fill it with compost. Nasturtiums flower best on poor soils, so adding one-third grit or perlite to your compost will reduce fertility and give you more flowers and smaller leaves. Using the compost as it is will still work, but will give you larger and lusher leaf growth and fewer flowers. If you plan to eat the leaves, or just like the idea of lots of lush foliage, this is maybe no bad thing.
3. Plant a few seeds in your hanging basket, by simply pushing them 1.5cm deep into the compost with a finger and covering them over. I like to sow 5 or 6 to make sure that I get some plants. If they all come up, you can thin out half the plants and eat them!
4. Water well and put the basket in a sunny position to get the best blooms.
5. Pick the flowers and leaves for salads, and try pickling the baby seed pods, which can be used like capers. Larger leaves can also be cooked like spinach, which removes their pepperiness, or even stuffed like vine leaves.

PROJECT: PLANT A POT OF CHAMOMILE TEA

Dried chamomile tea gives no clue to the amazingly zingy citrus fragrance of its fresh flowers and beautiful feathery foliage. Chamomile can be grown from seed, although some varieties are only available to buy as plants. The two main types for flowers are German, which is annual, and Roman, which is more often grown as a perennial.

When to do it:
Spring/summer.

Time from planting to harvest:
Approx. 10 weeks.

You will need:
Chamomile plants or seeds
A 30cm pot or larger
Peat-free multipurpose compost

If growing from seed:
A 9cm pot
Vermiculite (optional)

How to do it:
1. For a quick and easy project, buy yourself a chamomile plant from the garden centre. If you are willing to wait, grow from seed. The seeds are extremely tiny, so they should be sown on the surface of the soil in a 9cm pot and covered with a sprinkle of vermiculite or a very light dusting of soil. Early sowings are best germinated indoors in the warm. Once they are large enough

to handle, you can pot the seedlings up into individual pots to grow on, and harden them off before planting outside.
2. Make sure your pot has a drainage hole and optionally add some broken pots or gravel at the bottom. Fill with compost and plant your camomile plant in the centre of the pot.
3. Keep in a sunny position and water well. Chamomile grows rapidly, and you should have fragrant scented flowers in as little as 10 weeks from seed, or much sooner if you start with a plant.
4. To make a cup of chamomile tea, pop a few blooms into a cup of hot water and allow to infuse for 5 minutes. Remove the flowers after this or the tea can become bitter. To dry flowers to use for tea later, spread them out on some kitchen paper on a plate and leave in a sunny, wind-free spot outdoors, or in a well-ventilated place indoors, until dry, then store in a jar. You'll need fewer flowers for dried tea and the flavour will be different from fresh, so it's worth trying both.

PROJECT: MAKE A SUMMER CUT-FLOWER GARDEN

When I say make a cut-flower garden, I don't mean you need to designate a place just for flowers, but more just to remind you that a garden can be productive in more than just food. While I leave the majority of my flowers outdoors, I love to have cut flowers from the garden in my flat all summer long. They also make a lovely gift to a friend – I'm even growing my friend's wedding bouquet this year. Here are some suggestions for flowers to put in your garden and later your vases for plenty of colour all summer.

- **Brodiaea:** These perennial flowers are easy to grow and pop up year after year. I planted the little corms between rows of asparagus on my first ever allotment, and while my asparagus slowly got overcome by bindweed, the brodiaea came back stronger every year. It produces clusters of little blue flowers, a bit like a small agapanthus. It is planted in autumn for blooms the following summer.

- **Cosmos:** Cosmos are a must for me every year. They produce big delicate billowing plants with fine foliage and a huge number of beautiful flowers. They continue to flower right up until the first frost and make a great cut flower, as buds will happily open and flower after cutting and last for over a week in a vase. Sometimes I just throw a few seeds into a bed in late spring and let them do their thing. Otherwise I start them in pots or modules indoors in spring, to plant the little plug plants with a little more intention.

- **Dahlias:** Perhaps the ultimate cut flower, dahlias are stunning and come in so many colours and shapes. They may take a while to get going, often not flowering until mid- to late summer, but they carry on right up until the first frost. Dahlias are native to central America and were originally cultivated for their edible tubers. The tubers can be planted directly into a prepared garden bed when all risk of frost has passed, or started earlier in spring, in pots with some protection. Remove finished flowers to keep the plant producing more blooms. Simple open dahlias rather than elaborate ones with lots of petals are best for pollinators.

- **Gladioli:** If you want a spectacular and easy-to-grow summer flower, this is it. In colder areas gladioli may not survive the winter, but I have always left them in the ground – if they are happy they will come back larger each year and even produce lots of tiny bulbs underground around the corms. They like a sunny open spot, and you can simply dig a hole twice the depth of the bulb and pop them in. They may struggle if overcrowded by other tall plants, but otherwise bung them in and wait for their spectacular tall flower stems to burst into an array of beautiful gaudy colours. They are planted in spring for a summer display.

- **Zinnias:** Zinnias are bright showy flowers much loved by pollinators. You can sow them direct, where they can happily spring up with little attention, but I find mine often get gobbled up by slugs. So starting them off in modules and popping them out in a nice sunny spot will give you a better chance of success.

PROJECT: FILL YOUR FENCE WITH FLOWERS

Fences are prime real estate in a garden and in my mind they should be covered in plants. This gives the garden an abundant lush cocoon-like energy and is both way more attractive and better for wildlife than keeping a bare fence.

If you have a bare patch of fence, pick one of these great fence-filling, perennial flowering plants and start to surround yourself with lush foliage. These easy climbing and flowering plants all grow happily in my little garden.

- **Star jasmine (*Trachelospermum jasminoides*)** – I can't rave about this plant enough. On a recent trip to Rome I found it on every street, rambling across the fronts of beautiful brick buildings, but you don't need a Mediterranean climate to keep this extremely low-fuss glossy-leafed vine happy. It forms a carpet of evergreen leaves, which keeps fences covered all year round, and in late spring and summer it bursts into little white beautifully scented blossoms. Happiest in full sun, it can cope with a little shade – the main thing is to provide it support. Add some wires or strings to your fence or wall to help it find its way, as it likes to twine its stems. It can cope with pruning hard in spring, so if it's coming too far into the garden, just chop it back. It will eventually cover large areas but is slow-growing enough to keep in check to fill just the space you want it to.

- **Honeysuckle:** Honeysuckle is actually a big family of plants, including the edible honeyberry, which unlike a familiar climbing honeysuckle is a small fruiting bush. Climbing honeysuckle, which is best suited to covering fences, comes in many different varieties, including evergreen and deciduous ones. I have a beautiful yellow honeysuckle in my garden which loses all its leaves in winter before putting on fresh new shoots in spring. While it doesn't give winter cover, deciduous honeysuckle has the biggest and most abundant blooms and mine really does burst into flower, giving off the most incredible scent that drifts in through the windows. It also provides great cover for birds, which love to hop around inside it – insectivorous wrens particularly enjoy it while on the hunt for aphids.

- **Climbing roses:** Roses are an excellent way to fill a fence, bringing stunning blooms and, depending on the variety, gorgeous scent. You can use rose petals to make confetti and rosewater, dried in tea mixes or candied to decorate desserts. Different roses have different growth habits, and to cover a fence you'll want either a climbing or a rambling rose. Climbers tend to have larger flowers, grow more slowly and flower more than once in a season, while ramblers can be very vigorous and usually produce one huge flush of smaller flowers all in one go. You'll want to plant your rose in fertile soil next to a wall or fence for it to climb up, and ideally in a sunny spot, although the benefit of growing it on a fence is that even if the ground is a little in the shade, once the plant gets growing it can reach up into the light. Vertical wires along your fence will give you something to tie your rose to as it grows. In winter you can find bare-root plants, and potted ones are available all year round. They are best pruned in winter.

8

SIT BACK AND TAKE IT ALL IN

If you've done even one project, well done. Gardening doesn't have to be overwhelming. It is just about starting. Many of us struggle to find the confidence to try new things, when we don't think we know enough and we aren't sure where to start. Whatever the outcome, whatever the weather or the hungry critters have planned for your plants, I hope you have found pleasure in simply giving something a go. Perhaps you've even gained a new mindset, one where a garden is not a place of strict rules, of wrong and right or of success and failure, but a place to be enjoyed, to feed our imagination, to show us new and delightful things if we take the time to look.

Gardening is a great teacher of patience but also reminds us that things can suddenly come around quicker than we expect if we've simply found a moment to lay the groundwork. Many a time I have wished things would be ready faster, but the beauty of a garden is that everything has its moment, a rhythm, which we can all benefit from tuning into. And if you have started a project or two, sown some seeds or planted some bulbs, one day you'll walk out into your garden and find tulips blooming, fresh mint to pick, the first ripe tomato, or a frog sitting in a pond, and I really hope you take the time to relish the moment. This is just the beginning.

REMEMBER TO ENJOY YOUR GARDEN

It's easy to feel overwhelmed by how much there is to do in a garden, by the amount of clutter that can accumulate and the list of jobs to be done. Gardening is often a process that makes us feel better, but it's important to remember that a garden should not just be for gardening. Gardens are there to be enjoyed passively, just as they are to tend actively. To be seen and experienced. We are all more busy than ever, and it can be easy to forget to step out into your garden for days, weeks even, when there are a million more important things to do or the days are short and the temperature low. Here are some suggestions for how to get outside into the space you have so lovingly created.

1. Have a mini morning walkabout (with a cup of tea).
2. Have lunch in your garden, especially satisfying when it includes a few home-grown ingredients. The easiest thing I find for that is a few salad leaves!
3. Read a book in your garden.
4. Go and see what wildlife you can spot (worms and snails count), and remember to look closely and be curious. Make a note of what you see. Whenever I see a new critter I like to look it up so I know what it is next time I see it. In the last few weeks I've spotted a gorgeous stripey orange mining bee and a tiny baby green bush cricket with fabulous long antennae.
5. Pick some flowers for a vase; it's a great way to celebrate just a few blooms and still leave the rest in your garden.
6. Make tea from your garden – mint, rosemary, lemongrass, nettles and lemon leaves all make lovely tea!

7. Remember to take time to look at your plants, see what's changed and whether they need any help. Gardening is nurturing, and I've learned the most about plants by just paying attention to them.
8. Have a barbecue. Home-grown courgettes or even cucumbers are great on the barbecue. But don't let not having any produce to hand put you off. Just enjoy the surroundings.
9. Invite friends round on a warm summer evening and sit with a nice glass of something cold and some snacky bits.
10. Go out and scare a cat away when you see it trying to take a poo in your veg beds.
11. Chase a squirrel off your bird-feeder, or, as is often the case with me, if you find them too cute, just enjoy watching them instead, especially when they hang acrobatically upside down.
12. Perch somewhere and see if you can stay still long enough that birds will come and visit while you are there.
13. Munch your way around the garden – of course feel free to wash your produce first, but I enjoy picking a cucumber or a salad leaf, a fresh strawberry or a little tomato, a few pinkberries, and just eating them as I'm pottering around the garden.
14. Keep a little sun lounger on hand to unfold when the weather is nice and lie there just soaking up the sounds and sights of the garden for 15–20 minutes. Watch the birds that fly overhead and notice the bees buzzing among the flowers. Don't take your phone with you.

15. Invite a friend who likes plants over and potter about the garden, showing them proudly what you've been growing. Also have tea and cake, or wine.

Acknowledgements

Thanks first of all to my ever patient and attentive literary agent Ben for popping into my inbox one day and believing that I had a book in me and for helping me every step of the way.

Thanks to the wonderful team at Penguin: to Amy for allowing me to turn an idea into a reality and for always being on hand with reassurance and a listening ear, to Alice for her thoughtful notes and edits and to Annie for a very astute final eye, and last but not least to Nina for her gorgeous illustrations, which really bring the book to life.

To my dearly loved pals who always believe in me when I don't believe in myself, I could not have done it without you. A special thanks to my long-suffering housemate and dear friend Charlie, for agreeing to choose this flat for the garden and for letting me take it over.

To my girlfriend Georgia, who has really lived the many ups and downs of writing this book with me and always met me with a sympathetic ear and a great deal of patience. I love you.

To Catherine for those early morning chats about the book and for coming up with the name. Most of all thank you to my mum and dad, who have always loved me unconditionally, support me absolutely and have taken great pride in my many endeavours over the years. Especially to my mum, who brought me up surrounded by plants, a love of birds and a watchful eye. I hope to one day be half the gardener you are.

Index

acidic soil 213
alliums 232, 260
allotments 2, 57
annuals 33, 167–8
aphids 50, 55, 234, 250
apples 216–20
archways 7, 13, 24–5, 91, 269, 271
aubergines 148–52

baba ganoush recipe 151–2
balconies 4, 11, 18
bamboo canes 13, 25, 135–6
basil 162, 164, 167
beans, French 7, 91–8
   climbing 91–5
   dwarf 91, 96–8
beds, raised 58, 61–5, 198
beer traps 52–3
bees 169, 229–30, 232–4, 243, 260, 266–7
   drinking station for 236
beetles 229, 238
berries 211–12
biennials 33

biodiversity 230
birds 6, 54, 214, 229, 242–50
   feeding 230–2, 242–50
   planting for 243–4
black fly 55
blueberries 213–15
bolting 36
borage 232–3, 273–4
brodiaea 282
bulbs 259–68
   bulb lasagna 262–6
butterflies 6, 229, 232, 234
   cabbage white 53–4, 276

Caesar salad recipe 74–5
calendula 274
campion, red 234
canes 13, 25, 145–6
carrots 137–40
caterpillars 53–4, 130
cats 291
chamomile 279–81
chard 126–32
chemical pesticides 234
chervil 168

Chilean guava berries 211–12
chives 168
citrus 221–7
climate change 38–9
climbing plants 285–7
coir 19, 29
cold frames 16
   for spinach and radishes
      116–19
   see also greenhouses
comfrey tea 47–8
compost 15, 38, 38–41
   balancing
      ingredients 39–40
   bought 18–20, 29
   ericaceous 213
   making a wormery 41–5
   making potting mix 20
   re-using 23–4
container gardening
   choosing containers 143–4
   flower bulbs 262–6
   for fruit 211–15
   hanging baskets 82–4,
      276–825, 66, 198,
      266, 276–8
   for herbs 172–3, 174–7,
      181–3, 187–90
   for seed sowing 27–8
   strawberry tower 198–201
   for vegetables 65–6, 122–5,
      137–47, 162–5
coriander 168, 181–3
cornflowers 275

cosmos 282
cotoneaster 243
courgettes 46, 51, 66,
      107–12, 273
   barbecued with chilli,
      mint and feta recipe
      114–15
   courgette fritti recipe
      112–14
   hand-pollinating 111
crocuses 233, 260, 262, 265
cucumbers 100–6
cut-flowers 259, 269–72,
      282–4, 290
cuttings 10, 34
   figs 221
   mint 170–3
   rosemary 178–80
   tomatoes 89–90

daffodils (narcissus) 261,
      262, 265
dahlias 282
dandelions 243
deadheading 34, 265
deciduous plants 34
designing a garden 13–18
dill 168
Dowding, Charles 60
dragonflies 229
drainage 21–2

ericaceous compost 213
evergreens 34

INDEX

feeding plants 45–9
  homemade plant food 47–8
fennel 10
fertilizers 46
fig trees 221–3
  from cuttings 221
firming in 34
flower beds 14
flowers 259–87
  alliums 260
  borage 273–4
  brodiaea 282
  calendula 274
  chamomile 279–81
  climbing 285–7
  cornflowers 275
  cosmos 282
  cut-flowers 259, 269–72, 282–4, 290
  dahlias 284
  edible 273–81
  gladioli 284
  honeysuckle 286
  nasturtiums 276–8
  for pollinators 232–5, 274
  roses 286–7
  from seed 269–72
  spring bulbs 259–68
  spring flowering border 267–8
  star jasmine 285
  sweet peas 269–72
  zinnias 284
French beans 7, 91–8
  climbing 91–5
  dwarf 91, 96–8
frogs 229, 251
frost 145
fruit 195–227
  apples 216–20
  Chilean guava berries 211–12
  figs 221–3
  lemons 224–7
  pears 216–20
  physalis 207–10
  pink blueberries 213–15
  pollination 218
  in pots 211–12
  strawberries 196–206
  trees 216–20, 221–7
fungi 238
furniture 13–14

gardens, enjoying 289–91
garlic 162, 165
  flatbreads recipe 155–6
  greens 153–6
gladioli 284
grafting 35, 148, 216
grape hyacinths (muscari) 233, 260, 265
gravel gardens 191–3
greenhouses 8, 16, 148
greens 126–32
grit 20
grow bags 1, 66
guava berries 211–12

hand forks 12
hanging baskets 25, 66, 198, 266, 276–8
  for tomatoes 82–4
hardening off 32, 34
hardy plants 34
hedgehogs 229
herbs
  annual 167–8
  basil 162, 164, 167
  chamomile 279–81
  chervil 168
  chives 168
  in containers 187–90
  coriander 168, 181–3
  dill 168
  propagating from supermarket herbs 170–7, 184–6, 187–90
  lavender 191
  lemongrass 174–7
  marjoram 191
  Mediterranean gravel garden 191–3
  mint 168, 170–3
  oregano 168–9, 191–3
  parsley 168, 184–6
  perennial 168–9
  rosemary 169, 178–80
  sage 169, 191
  thyme 169, 191–3
hoes 12–13
honeysuckle 233, 286

hoverflies 232
hyacinths 260

insects
  declining numbers 230
  pests 50, 53–5, 234, 250, 276
  pollinators 169, 229–36, 284, 243, 260, 266–7
irises 261
irrigation 23
ivy 244

jasmine, star 285

kale 57, 126–30
Kew Gardens 1–2

lacewings 232
ladybirds 55
lavender 191, 233
lawns 16
  flowering 235
  removing 7
layout of a garden 13–18
leaf miners 54–5
leaves
  cotyledons 35
  leaf mould 38
  leaf piles 238
  true leaves 35–6
lemongrass 174–7
lemons 224–7
lentil greens 157–9
  red lentil dal recipe 160–1

INDEX

light levels 17–18
log piles 229, 238–41

mangetout 133–6
marjoram 191
Mediterranean herb
    garden 191–3
melons 116
microgreens 157–9
mint 168, 170–3
module trays 27–8
moths 229, 232
mulch 23, 24
multipurpose compost 18–19
    for seed sowing 29

narcissus 261, 262
nasturtiums 276–8
nature watching 230–2, 242,
    251, 256–7, 290
nematodes 52
netting plants 54, 214
nettle tea 47
New Zealand 4
no-dig beds 38, 60–2
nutrients 45–6

onions, spring 122–5
oregano 168–9, 191–3

parsley 168, 184–6
paths, making 58–60
patios 13
peas 133–6

perennials 33
    flowers 234
    herbs 168–9
perlite 20, 29
pesticides 234
pests
    aphids 50, 55, 234, 250
    birds 54, 201
    cabbage white butterflies
        53–4, 276
    caterpillars 53–4, 130
    leaf miners 54–5
    managing 49–55
    pesticides 49
    slugs and snails 50–2,
        73, 119
physalis 207–10
pigeons 54
pinching out 35
pink blueberries 213–15
pollination 111, 218
    attracting pollinating insects
        232–3, 284
polytunnels 16
ponds 229
    choosing a location 251
    mini wildlife pond 251–7
    plants for 253
potatoes 141–6
    boiling 146
    breakfast röstis
        recipe 146–7
    chitting 28, 144
    varieties 141–3

pots 18–19
    flower bulbs in 262–6
    fruit in 211–15
    herbs in 172–3, 181–3
    re-potting 36, 226
    rootbound plants 36
    for seed sowing 28
    storing 25
    strawberry tower 198–201
    vegetables in 7, 65–6,
        122–5, 137–40, 162–5
potting mix 20
potting up 32
pricking out 35
primroses 233
propagating
    from cuttings 10, 34, 89–90,
        170–3, 178–80, 221
    from runners 202–3
    grafting 35, 148, 216
    from seeds 1, 26–32, 35,
        66–7, 79–81
    from supermarket herbs
        170–7, 184–6
propagators 30
pruning 35, 220
    cordons 87

radishes 116–19
    pickled 120–1
raised beds 58, 61–3, 198
    filling cheaply 63–5
recipes
    any greens pasta 131–2

baba ganoush 151–2
barbecued courgettes with
    chilli, mint and feta
    114–15
breakfast röstis 146–7
Caesar salad 74–5
chamomile tea 281
courgette fritti 112–14
garlic flatbreads 155–6
pickled radishes 120–1
red lentil dal 160–1
recycling 28
rented homes 6
rosemary 169
    from cuttings 178–80
roses, climbing 286–7

sage 169, 191
salad leaves 69–75, 116, 162–3
salvia 'Hot Lips' 234
seating 13–14, 18
secateurs 12
seeds 1
    containers for 27
    growing from 26–31, 224
    how to sow 29–31
    light and heat 31
    potting up seedlings 32
    sowing indoors 26
    sowing outdoors 27,
        35, 66–7
    tomatoes 79–81
    watering 30
shade 7, 17–18

INDEX

sheds 15
shelves 25–6
slugs 50–2, 73, 119
   watching 229–30
snails 50–2, 73, 119
soil
   acidic 213
   fertility 38
   preparing 60–1
   taking care of 37–8
soil-based compost 19
spades 12
spinach 116–19, 162
   perpetual 126–32
spring onions 122–5
squirrels 247, 291
   protecting bulbs from 264, 268
stag beetles 238
star jasmine 285
strawberries 196–206
   containers for 198–201
   wild 204–6
stumpery 241
successional planting 162–5, 181
sunflowers 244
sunny areas 17–18
sustainability 16, 38
sweet peas 7, 269–72
sweet potatoes 116

tea, from your garden 279–81, 290

teasel 244
teepees 25, 135–6
tender plants 33
thyme 169, 191–3
tomatoes 77–90, 162–4
   in hanging baskets 82–4
   making free plants 89–90
   from seed 79–81
   vining 85–8
tools 12–13
transplanting 36
trees
   apples and pears 216–20
   buying 216–17
   figs 221–3
   lemons 224–7
   in pots 216–20
trowels 12
tulips 261, 262
twine 13

valerian 234
vegetables 14, 17
   best spots for growing 58
   buying plants 148
   carrots 137–40
   courgettes 107–15
   cucumbers 100–6
   decorative 57
   edible flowers 273–81
   French beans 91–8
   garlic 162, 165
   garlic greens 153–6
   making beds for 58

vegetables – *cont'd*
  mangetout 133–6
  peas 133–6
  potatoes 141–7
  in pots 65–6
  radishes 116–21
  salad leaves 69–75, 162–3
  spinach 116–19, 162
  spring onions 122–5
  successional planting 162–5
  tomatoes 77–90, 162–4
vermiculite 20, 29
vertical growing 24–5, 285–7
  salad 70–1

wallflowers 233
watering 22–3, 145
  collecting rainwater 15–16
  seeds 30
waterlogging 21

weeds 3, 12, 14, 23, 60–2, 94–5
wildlife gardening 2, 7–8, 11, 14, 229–57
  attracting birds 230–2, 242–50
  bee drinking station 236
  log piles 238–41
  mini wildlife ponds 251–7
  pollinators 232–5
  watching wildlife 230–2, 242, 251, 256–7, 290
wind protection 116
window boxes 25, 66, 104–6
windowsill gardening 153–9, 177
woodlice 229
wormeries, making 41–5

zinnias 284